MAY I HAVE THE PLEASURE?

THE STORY OF POPULAR DANCING

This edition published by arrangement with BBC Books,
a division of BBC Enterprises Ltd

MAY I HAVE THE
PLEASURE?

THE STORY OF POPULAR DANCING

Written by Belinda Quirey
with Steve Bradshaw and Ronald Smedley

Illustrated by Illustra Design Ltd.

Edited by Libby Halliday

DANCE BOOKS   CECIL COURT   LONDON

Belinda Quirey, who is a founder fellow (and past Chairman) of the Historical Branch of the Imperial Society of Teachers of Dancing, lectures in dance history at the Royal Academy of Dancing, the London College of Dance and Drama, the London Academy of Music and Dramatic Art, Elmhurst Ballet School and the University of York, Department of Music.

Steve Bradshaw, after studying English at Queens College, Cambridge, joined BBC Radio London during its early days, producing and presenting 'Breakthrough' a rock magazine programme for young people. Now a freelance journalist, broadcaster and disc-jockey, he writes regularly for 'New Society', and is a reporter on the BBC Radio 1 'Newsbeat' programme.

Ronald Smedley is Producer of the series 'May I Have The Pleasure?', a member of the English Folk Dance and Song Society and visiting teacher in traditional dance at the Royal Ballet School.

First published by the British Broadcasting Corporation in 1976

© The authors and the British Broadcasting Corporation 1976

This edition published in 1987 by Dance Books Ltd., 9 Cecil Court, London WC2N 4EZ

Distributed in the USA by Princeton Book Co., P.O. Box 109, Princeton, N.J. 08540

British Library Cataloguing in Publication Data
Quirey, Brenda
  May I have the pleasure? : the story of popular dancing.
  1. Dancing
  I. Title   II. Bradshaw, Steve   III. Smedley, Ronald
  IV. Halliday, Libby
  793.3   GV1601

ISBN 1-85273-000-5

Design and production in association with
Book Production Consultants, 47 Norfolk Street, Cambridge

Printed and bound by The Burlington Press (Cambridge) Limited, Foxton, Cambridge

Contents

'We have interpreted the word "popular", not in the old strict sense of the "people" as opposed to the "patricians", but in a sense that seems to be more rewarding and fruitful when we are dealing with dancing. "Popular" we have taken to mean the trend-setting level in any particular age, where the action was, where the new developments took place. This takes us admittedly to court level and aristocratic style between the 12th and the 18th century. But in the 19th century we find ourselves dealing with dance at the level of the bourgeoisie, and today we are happily back with a universal dance-form.'

⌘ Sections following and preceding this symbol are technical descriptions of steps or techniques, or technical matter. The reader may omit these sections without losing the sense of the chapter. ⌘

* Refer to Glossary.

Introduction

'What a charming amusement for young people this is, Mr Darcy! There is nothing like dancing after all. I consider it one of the first refinements of polished societies.'

'Certainly, sir; and it has the advantage also of being in vogue amongst the less polished societies of the world. Every savage can dance.'

Pride and Prejudice. Jane Austen.

If we try to understand what dancing was like before the age of cinematography and sound recording we find we have to rely on evidence that is always inadequate and may be misleading. Let us imagine that we receive from an overseas friend a packet of still photographs, some sheet music, and a description in words of a dance he has composed for us. If we are to rely on these materials alone, what are our chances of recreating the dance exactly?

They will depend on whether we have a common technique, such as classical ballet, with a terminology known to both of us; on whether the music has a metronome marking, and is in a familiar dance rhythm; and on whether we share at least some fundamental assumptions about human movements and dancing. If none of these conditions is fulfilled the odds against a correct reconstruction are long.

None of these conditions *is* fulfilled when we come to the dances of former ages, particularly of those earlier than the 19th century. We have a great deal of pictorial, musical and verbal evidence, but our results will depend on the interpretation we put on it. Here we are at the mercy of our present-day preconceptions and predilections. If we are not to be led astray by these – often unrecognized and unexamined – prejudices, we must first establish what actual data we are given in each kind of evidence and what are the justifiable inferences we can make from these.

Pictorial evidence consists of all the paintings, drawings, tapestries, and sculpture that show us dancing figures. Even at their most communicative they can give us only static positions or groupings, and something of the muscle tensions and 'tone' of the individual bodies. We have to infer the most likely transitional movement between any two positions; in reproducing the particular body 'tone' portrayed we must rely on empathy*, a sense that as a rule today is poorly developed in Western man.

We have to make allowances both for the style of draughtmanship in different ages, and the methods of reproduction that were available before our present sophisticated techniques. Good examples of illustrations that can mislead us badly are the drawings in Thoinot Arbeau's Orchesography (1588). This is one of the most deservedly popular books on old dancing, written by a Canon of Langres, who pretends that he is giving instructions to an imaginary pupil called Capriol. Capriol is represented as a quaint little woodcut figure, endearing and unpretentious, and very badly drawn; in some of the figures it is hard to tell which leg is which. The impression we get is homely, folksy and disarming.

But the dances which Arbeau is describing are the great dances of the High Renaissance: Pavane, Galliard, Almain, and Coranto. We shall never understand what Pavane should be like if we associate it with this little creature. We have to imagine in his place the figures of Leicester, Sidney, Raleigh, and Essex in all their splendour and magnificence – quite a trap for the unwary as you can see.

Reproduction of the figures in a painting by a woodcut of it can alter entirely the atmosphere of the original. Below we see a famous picture of a couple

Top left: 'Capriol' from Arbeau's Orchesography.

Left: Sir Walter Raleigh (Artist unknown).

Above: Queen Elizabeth dancing la volta with the Earl of Leicester.

Right: Bal à La Cour des Valois (Chateau de Blois).

dancing a Volta, often thought to be Queen Elizabeth with the Earl of Leicester (there are actually several paintings, slightly different, and the identity of the dancers has caused much controversy among art historians). If we try to reconstruct the dance from the woodcut, without a previous knowledge of the painting, we shall be aiming at quite a wrong style, far too 'quaint', and in this case almost grotesque. And of course with any engraving we have to remember that right and left are transposed.

There are in addition many artistic conventions, too numerous and too subtle to deal with here but presenting peculiar hazards for the uninitiated.

Finally we have to cope with figures which, while seeming to be far more skilfully drawn than poor little Capriol, contain anatomical impossibilities. The most flagrant of these occurs in one of our most famous publications, Carlo Blasis' Elementary Treatise of 1820. This is of crucial importance to us for it is the first real evidence of ballet technique as we know it today. The young man

Left: Illustration from Carlo Blasis 'Elementary Treatise'.
Illustration by Randolph Schwabe from 'The Manual of Classical Theatrical Dancing – Cecchetti Method'.

posing for the technical illustrations would appear to have no bony hip girdle. He is shown in a position which no human body could achieve.

Exactly the same mistake was repeated over a century later in another book of fundamental importance to historians: The Manual of Classical Theatrical Dancing – Cecchetti Method. This gives us the system taught by Diaghilev's great ballet master, Enrico Cecchetti. The faulty illustrations of both these books have added to the confusion about the unusual position of the legs throughout classical ballet.

When we come to musical evidence we, as dancers, have to rely on the results of the study of old music notations by musicologists. This in itself presents certain risks. Until quite recently most musicologists hardly knew that dancing existed, at least as a subject to be taken seriously. Their interests lay in the mathematical study of polyphony, counterpoint, and harmony, in differing modes and scales, and in varying sonorities and timbres. Within the last ten or fifteen years all this has changed. We have even what might be called early pop groups. Many young men take an interest in playing the more unusual old instruments. But their sense of rhythm is still very unreliable. There is hardly one commercial recording of old music that can be danced to satisfactorily. If they themselves try to perform the dances they usually dance them too badly to be of any use as a guide for their playing. Some of the instruments, too, are so difficult even to keep in tune that little thought and energy is left to achieve the proper rhythm. And with some of the instruments no control of dynamics is possible, only of duration and pitch.

What musical evidence does give us is the form of the dance as a whole – binary, ternary, rondeau form etc.,* and the particular rhythmic unit – galliard, minuet, polka step and so on. We are left to infer the tempo (Stravinsky's 'single most important factor in music') and all the subtleties of flow and phrasing.

What must be emphasized is that if the description and execution of old dance movements are to be used as a guide to the tempo of old music, then it is essential that they should be reconstructed correctly and performed by bodies of both great elasticity and strength. These are rare birds. Our professionals are strong enough but they lack the required elasticity in their feet and legs; most amateurs lack the strength in their backs and legs and tend to be either stiff or sloppy. All of us today have our centre of gravity several inches too far back for the pre-19th century techniques.

With verbal evidence we have a stumbling-block that has tripped up nearly all of our would-be dance historians. Many of the names used in descriptions of old dances are familiar to many dancers today – coupés, chassés, bourrées, contretemps, and a great many more. The trouble is that the movements are different from the ones we know today by those names. ('Names remain, but substance changes.') Sometimes they are completely different as with coupés and chassés sometimes different in detail as with bourrées.

In describing general movement qualities, too, or even a simple specific movement, words are liable to wide misinterpretation. Anyone who fails to realize this should ask a mixed group of gymnasts and ballet students to bend their knees. The different responses should soon settle the question.

The shortcomings of these three kinds of evidence – pictorial, musical and verbal – are often given as a reason for relying on the old dance notations. Of course the use of a good, and suitable, movement notation is the answer to many problems of recording and communication today. But their advocates overlook the real difficulty when we are dealing with techniques which are no longer alive, and with the notations that recorded some of them. We have no decoding clerk at hand to demonstrate to us what movements their symbols referred to. The key to the notation is itself in *words*. So evidence from old notations reduces to verbal evidence, with all its limitations and ambiguities.

(The one exception to this impasse is the diagrams of the floor-tracks in Feuillet's Stenochoregraphy (1700); these are purely graphic and of inestimable value to our understanding of Baroque dance form.)

Faced with such a minefield of hazards how can we avoid misinterpreting the evidence as many would-be dance historians have been doing for so long? There is really only one solution. We must become as familiar with the background and beliefs of the age we are studying as we are with the mental climate of our own day. It is worse than useless to pore over the documents extracting just the bits of information that make sense to our post-Romantic present-day viewpoint. Nor is anything to be gained by approaching the matter purely cerebrally: this will result in mere pedantry.

What is needed is the imaginative willingness to embrace principles and standards that at first sight seem utterly foreign to us: Mediaeval courtesy, Renaissance Platonism, the aristocratic and mathematical outlook of the 17th and 18th centuries. All these could hardly be farther from our present approach to dancing. Yet only by widening our horizons, by stretching and strengthening the muscles of our minds to these Olympic standards, can we hope to enter this hitherto neglected and richly rewarding field of our Western heritage.

From our roots to the Renaissance

The roots

Western dancing is quite different from Oriental dancing; different too from such primitive dance styles as we can still find in undeveloped countries today. It is possible that we once garbed ourselves in fur, feathers, and even grass skirts, and cavorted about, shaking our torsos and waving our arms to the frenetic beating of drums and tom-toms. But within historical time a very different picture emerges. When old Western man wanted to dance he held out his hands to his fellows, and they all joined together in a linked line and sang.

Not percussion, therefore, but the melodic phrase is the rhythmic basis of our dancing. The nearest we get to a percussive rhythm is the transferring of our weight from foot to foot on the pulse of the music. What seems as a rule to have been avoided was any unnecessary expenditure of muscular energy by stamping, or beating, or banging our feet on the ground.

A similar economy of effort can be seen in our arm and body movements. We never in the West make the symbolic arm and hand gestures that are characteristic of so much Eastern, particularly Indian, dancing. The body, though never stiff, remains controlled and upright, with no writhing or contorted movements, and the head and shoulders, while turning freely and flexibly, are always level and never sink down or incline to the side.

These qualities, depending on our viewpoint, can be seen as either limitations or virtues. They are almost certainly the result of our linked arms and communal feeling in the old chain formation, the root of all our serious dancing until the end of the 18th century. Once out of the chain our arms are used mainly to balance us, and our vertical axis departs from the upright only as we bank slightly when travelling round a curve.

The two rhythms of Western dancing echo the basic rhythms of our bodies, our heart-beat and our breathing. Our feet coming down on the metrical beat make the same type of rhythm as our pulse. And above this base our upper bodies respond to the phrases of the melody with the free-flowing arc of our breathing. This combination results in a dance form which has both great mechanical economy and physiological ease.

Carole

The chain-dance is very old, possibly as old as the height of Minoan civilization in Crete (c. 1400–1200 B.C.). This would mean that it has been danced for more than three thousand years. It is certainly as old as Homer, for he makes it one of the items on the Shield of Achilles in the Eighteenth Book of the Iliad. He describes it there in its two main forms – circular and linear.

The true circular dance, the Ring Dance, is probably the oldest of all Western dance forms. It usually had a central focus, a sacred object such as a tree or a standing stone, to which the whole dance was aimed, the dancers moving in towards and away from it. But this form had no major developments in our history, nor is it the kind of circle dance that Homer describes. We mention it here merely to establish that it existed. The English Country Dance Sellenger's Round is a perfect example of it.

Apollo and the Muses by Giulio Romano.
How the Renaissance imagined the ancient Ring Dance.

When we come upon the chain-dance in the early Middle Ages it is called the Carole. It still has two different forms, circular and linear, as in Homer, the linear form being called Farandole. The circular form, which was not a Ring Dance but could be done equally well in an arc of a circle, was called a Branle. Farandole appears to have been characteristic of the Mediterranean countries, while Branles were popular in more northern climes.

Farandole
In Farandole we have a linked line of dancers moving forwards as they sing. They can move to any music so long as it is metrical, i.e. that it has a regular pulse. It can be in duple or triple time, simple or compound; it makes no difference. To their singing the dancers can walk, or run, or what we call today 'skip': 'skipping' means that we take a walking step with one foot and then hop on it, repeating this 'step and hop' with alternate feet. The rhythm, provided it keeps to the regular pulse, is immaterial.

What is important in Farandole is the pattern the line of dancers makes in space; we call this the 'Figure'. The Figures in Farandole are all very simple ones. The easiest of all is just a labyrinthine track over the floor, curving round, twisting and turning back on itself, apparently at random. It is the leader of the

Miniature of Round Dance before the God of Love by the Master of the Roman de la Rose. Mediaeval French Branle at its most characteristic.

line who is responsible for this pattern and this is the source of the phrase 'He led us a fine dance', now used only metaphorically.

'. . . the dancer greatest praise hath won
Which with best order can all orders shun;
For everywhere he wantonly must range
And turn and wind with unexpected change.'

from Orchestra by Sir John Davies 1596.

This was written in the late 16th century about a dance called Coranto which was the late Renaissance development from Farandole.

The most characteristic Figures in Mediaeval Farandole are three arched ones: the first two of these have single arches and are called 'Threading the Needle' and 'L'Escargot' (the Snail); the third has multiple arches and no special name, so we will just call it 'The Arches'.

1 *Threading the Needle*

※ The leader steps across to face the second dancer and they raise their joined hands so that their arms make a single arch (not a double-arm arch like the game of Oranges and Lemons). The third dancer breaks hands with the second and goes through the arch drawing the remainder of the line after him and becoming the new leader. As the last dancer goes through the arch he takes the hand of the former leader who goes under his own raised arm to become the penultimate dancer in the new line. The former second dancer is now last in the line.

The new leader can now do another 'Thread the Needle', at the end of which No. 5 will be the head of the dance, and so on all down the line. If there is an even number of dancers in the line only the odd-numbered ones will have a turn at leading before we get back to our original first dancer; but if there is an odd number everyone will have a turn before the first leader gets back to his original place. ✻

2 *L'Escargot (The Snail)*
✻ Here the first dancer leads the line into a spiral pattern until he is right in the middle, and the line is coiled round and outwards from him, like the shell of a snail. He then turns to face the second dancer, but they do not make a static arch as in 'Threading the Needle'. Keeping firm hold of her hand he throws her arm back over her head; she goes under her own arm, turns a half turn away from the leader, and both of them walk back down the line, one on each side of it, as the line itself goes under the arch and follows her round. No one breaks their hand-hold in l'Escargot, and both the arch and the line move – and in opposite directions – as opposed to 'Threading the Needle' where only the lines moves. We do not get a change of leader in l'Escargot. ✻

3 *The Arches*
✻ The leader draws the dancers out into a straight line, or an easy curve, where they all turn sideways and raise their arms into a series of arches. The leader goes under the arch between No. 2 and No. 3 from front to back, and through the arch between No. 3 and No. 4 from back to front, and so on leading the whole line cumulatively after him. Turning into the moving line is easy for the even numbers who just have to bend slightly forward and follow on; the odd numbers have a harder time for they have to make a backwards turn. This is a highly decorative Figure and is seen in a good many ballets, most outstandingly in Les Sylphides. ✻

In the late Middle Ages all these arched Figures disappeared from Farandole. It is always difficult to establish exactly when something ceased to be popular, but assuming that it was during the 15th century that these fell into disuse, then it may have been because of the women's elaborate head-dresses that were in vogue. Both the hennin, the pointed hat like a dunce's cap, and the double-horned head-dress, in which actresses tend to look like sacred cows, are a hazard to an arched figure in a dance. Whatever the cause the raised arm had completely disappeared from upper-class dancing by the early 16th century. It remained, of course, a characteristic feature of all peasant work. We do not see it at Court again until the second half of the 18th century in a dance called Alle-mande. (NOT the Renaissance Allemande or Almain: quite a different dance.) This is very important to remember if one wants a theatrical production to look authentic, especially as old-fashioned producers tend to think of the raised arm as the essence of 'Courtly style'. As a help to our memory in preventing stylistic errors we could say that from the last hope of the Plantagenets (Perkin Warbeck, hanged 1499), to the last hope of the Stuarts (Bonnie Prince Charlie, Culloden 1746) arms at Court must never be higher than shoulder level.

There may have been a much more subtle reason for the disappearance of these arches. They almost certainly had a symbolic significance to earlier ages. They represented going through a gateway into an after-world. These beliefs linger on implicitly at a subconscious level long after they have been explicitly repudiated. Finally, however, they lose even this hold. That may have happened here. We simply do not know.

Once the arched Figures are removed from Farandole we are left with the original labyrinthine track and the unarched Figure. This is the Hey (Hay, Heye, or Haye). The fundamental importance of this Figure in Western dance form can hardly be exaggerated: it is the root of all our spatial design in dancing until the time of Romantic Ballet when quite other elements took over. Basically a Hey is the changing of the dancers' location in relation to each other. The Grand Chain in an Eightsome Reel or the Lancers is the simplest example. The dancers pass each other by alternate right and left shoulders as the men progress round a circle anti-clockwise and the girls clock-wise. This is a circular Hey. It can be done by as few as four people, or by as many as the available space can accommodate round its circumference. (Theoretically by the entire population of the world Heying round the Equator!)

The type of Hey that was originally in Farandole was a linear one. It occurred probably when two lines met each other, say in a forest clearing, and 'Heyed' through each other, reforming into their original linked file formation as they emerged from each end of the Hey. There are innumerable types of linear Hey. The smallest possible is for three dancers, a figure of eight on the floor being traced by all of them simultaneously, each starting at a different point: this is a Reel of Three. A Reel of Four has an extra loop to the figure eight, and from then on we get more and more possible combinations of curves and passes. These Heys are the basis of Italian Renaissance Danze and Balli, and of the fascinating floor-tracks of the English Country Dance.

'My men, like satyrs grazing on the lawns,
Shall with their goat feet dance an antic hay,'

says Marlow in his Edward II (1593). The 'antic' here has both the meaning of 'grotesque' (for his 'men' are his group of professional buffoons), and 'antique', very old; in fact the very old non-arched Figure of Farandole.

Branles

The circular form of Mediaeval Carole is not an essential Round Dance, a form which requires a complete and unbroken ring of dancers. The chain of dancers in a Branle can, and often did, join up into a Round, but all Branles can equally well be performed in an arc of a circle.

The early French 'branler' means to sway. Many dance teachers have interpreted this as meaning that each dancer sways about rather like the swooning bodies in pre-Raphaelite paintings. But this is a mistake. The 'sway' is much more like the swing of a pendulum, and it means the travelling from side to side of the whole linked line going first to the left and then to the right.

Whereas Farandole bequeathed us simple figures as its contribution to later dance form, Branles gave us rhythms. Very simple rhythms to start with, which were expressed in our characteristic Western way of transferring our body weight from foot to foot. In Farandole this was just a regular walking, or running, or skipping step, but in Branles we get a rhythmic pattern of quick and slow steps or of varying jumps and hops.

The common Suite of Branles consisted of Branle Double, Branle Simple, and Branle Gai. There was also a very important fourth Branle, later known as Branle de Bourgogne.

1 *Branle Double*

Branle Double is the source of probably the most important rhythm in the whole of dance history in the West, for it gives us the eight-bar phrase. Until recently this was so fundamental a phrase-length that many students would have thought of it as a fact of Nature. Nearly all hymn tunes and popular songs consist of phrases of this length, as does of course Ballad-metre. The Ballad was originally a dance-song.

⁂ The dancers in Branle Double take three steps to the left (L. R. L.) and on the fourth count either pause or close the right foot up to the left one; then they repeat this with the opposite foot going to the right. This combined step of three weight changes and a pause or close is called a 'Double'. It is not so much a 'step', in the sense of a ballet jeté or assemblé, as a measure of time; it can be divided into two 'Simples', or 'Singles', each of which is one step and a close. The two Simples give us the rhythm 'slow, slow', which is a Spondee in the scansion of Greek and Latin verse. The Double, as a rule, gives us the rhythm 'quick, quick, slow', an Anapaest in Classical prosody.* The Double can on occasion reverse this Anapaest and use the rhythm 'slow, quick, quick', which is a Dactyl. The relation of quick to slow in these is the very simple ratio of 1:2.

When Victor Silvester used to say 'Slow, slow, quick, quick, slow' I used to wonder how many of his audience realized we were reliving the exact rhythms of the Chorus in so many Greek tragedies, two and a half thousand years ago. ⁂

2 *Branle Simple*

⁂ In Branle Simple the line makes a Double to the left, but only a Simple back to the right. This gives us the rhythm 'quick, quick, slow, slow', and a six-bar phrase, divided not into two threes, but into four and two.

Dances based on Branle Simple with a six-bar phrase are nearly always lighter and more interesting than those with unrelieved, square, eight-bar phrases. Unfortunately nearly all dances tend to regress to the old eight-bar phrase pattern as they get older. ⁂

3 *Branle Gai*

⁂ In Branle Gai we leave walking in slow and quick steps and take to springing. To a count of 6 we spring with alternate feet (L. R. L. R.) on 1, 2, 3 and 4, and pause for the beats 5 and 6. Then we repeat this exactly, with the same foot, continuing to the left and not, in this Branle, going back to the right at all.

If the essence of a Branle is the movement of the line to one side and then to the other, the third main example of the form breaks this basic rule. How like life! If we were making this up instead of trying to find out what really happened, how much tidier we could have made it all.

This six-beat rhythm is of fundamental importance in the Middle Ages and the Renaissance. It was the root of Tordion, Salterello, Galliard, and Volta, and the main springing rhythm for five hundred years. Then it died, in the early 17th century, and disappeared entirely from serious dancing.

It is usually played so badly today that we may be allowed to utter a word of warning: it is *not* two bars of waltz-time. To dance it properly we need the first three beats all to be strong, not 'strong, weak, weak' as in Waltz, and the fourth beat to be very strong indeed. It is the neglect of the second beat (at least in the odd-numbered bars), in the playing of old triple-time rhythms, that makes it difficult to dance them today. ✷

4 *Branle de Bourgogne* (the Renaissance name)
✷ Here we go back to the eight-stress phrase of Branle Double, but have for the first time a step with a mixture of walking and springing. It is what most children call a Polka, step, step, step, hop, on four even beats. This is not a real Polka of course, which has an extra spring and a dotted note in the rhythm, compared with this easy 'one, two, three, hop'. But it is a popular step and one finds it cropping up again and again in duple-time dances. This is its early root. ✷

There were many other Branles. The form became the basis of French Folk dance, and by the 16th century every province and locality in France seemed to sport its own speciality. These folk forms often included mime, sometimes of working actions, e.g. The Washerwomen's Branle, Le Branle des Lavandières. But for our purposes of tracing development it is the four early examples that are important, for they are the rhythmic sources of nearly all our dancing until the end of the Renaissance, and most notably three of the four main High Renaissance dances, Pavane, Galliard, and Almain; only the fourth, Coranto, is derived directly from Farandole, without a rhythmic root in an old Branle.

Note on pronunciation: The English called Branles, Brauls or Brawls, and there were no doubt occasions when they became brawls in the modern sense (though the etymology is disputed here; the word may come from a different root). For the most part, however, we have no reason to think that they were not perfectly seemly. This is merely an example of the usual English unwillingness to adjust our tongues to the niceties of foreign phonetics – a fine Churchillian disregard for such things.

Courtly love

The emergence of Estampie

How did we ever get ourselves out from the Carole line? Today it is taken for granted on social occasions that a man should dance with a woman; but that has been the norm for less than the last nine hundred years. We think that the change must have occurred in Provence in the 12th century, and that it was due to the influence of Courtly Love.

Courtly Love was a very strange European phenomenon which has had a fundamental effect on our Western imagination. One tends at first to dismiss it as a mere literary convention, comparable with the conventions in the classic detective story today, but it was much more than that. C. S. Lewis in The Allegory of Love and Denis de Rougemont in Passion and Society both explain it brilliantly. From our dancing point of view the Troubadours, the love-songs, the adoration of the Lady gave us one important thing – the couple dance.

In early Mediaeval Provence this was called an Estampie. (No, it doesn't mean a stamping dance.) One of two things must have happened.

1 The men and the girls in the Carole line may have broken the chain and joined up into pairs. Then they formed a procession, one couple behind another, rather like a schoolgirls' crocodile, and all danced at the same time round the circumference of the dancing-floor. This is 'Processional' dance, and though it can be a very stately dance form it is not necessarily so. Barn Dance and the Lambeth Walk are both processional dances.

2 The alternative theory to this is more interesting and, seen in the light of subsequent history, more likely. Let us imagine the scene in the Provençal garden where, in the Mediterranean sunshine, the Carole line is dancing a Branle. Out from the chain dance steps one couple. They are side by side with the woman on the man's right, as they would have been as the first two dancers in the Branle. They dance *alone*, to the Branle air, going forward and backwards where the Branle went left and right, and making a few rudimentary figures. Their friends who had been dancing the Carole with them stand or sit around looking on.

This is the Danse à Deux. Obviously this always means a dance for two, but used in our specialised sense it is not an ordinary couple dance, with a number of couples performing at the same time. The one couple who are dancing have the whole of the dancing-floor to themselves (this is very important), and they dance both for their own enjoyment and for that of their watching friends.

If this true Danse à Deux did not come into being in 12th-century Provence, then it must have been born in Lombardy or Tuscany at some time in the following two centuries, for in Northern Italy by the 1400s it is taken completely for granted as the accepted dance form. There are some communal dances as well, but the most important dances at any gathering (above the folk level) were performed one couple, or one set, at a time, with the whole of the dance floor to themselves. This way of dancing spread to the rest of Europe and became the normal order of things right up to the latter half of the 18th century.

But Provence and the scene of the Troubadours was far the most likely birthplace for this unique dance-form. Psychologically too the Danse à Deux fits the facts and the situation better than does the Processional form. So let us assume, for our purposes here, that the Estampie *was* a Danse à Deux.

Unfortunately we know very little about Estampies apart from their music. This in itself marks a great progression for it is instrumental music in contrast to the singing in Carole. Secondly it has a finite form, a beginning, a middle, and an end, whereas in Carole, as in Ballroom dancing today, the music could theoretically go on for ever. This applies particularly to Farandole; when a Branle was being danced to a narrative ballad, sung perhaps by a minstrel with the dancers joining in with him on the chorus lines, the end of the story would obviously mean the end of the music and the dance. But the ballad would consist only of the verse tune repeated again and again; it would not have any progressive musical form.

The most important difference between an Estampie and Carole is the spatial one: an Estampie is oriented, it has a *front*. Carole, again like our Ballroom dancing today, mills round and round with no specific focus. Estampies are focused directly forward to the Presence, the Lord or the Lady or, if they themselves are dancing, to the place where they would have been. This marks a stage of enormous importance: it is probably the first time in our history that dancing has had a human focus. All serious dancing in classical antiquity was addressed to a god, or his altar. The Pantomimus in ancient Rome certainly had a human audience but what he was performing was a type of narrative mime, not pure dance. The Roman Mimi were a mixture of acrobats and knockabout comedians and cannot begin to be included here. As for the chorus in Greek tragedy, their dancing was unquestionably serious, and almost certainly pure dance, but the presence of the altar on the orchestra (the orchestra was the dancing-floor) establishes the presence of the superhuman.

But with Estampies we appear to have had serious dancing addressed to a human Presence. This was not mere entertainment. That was provided by the buffoons, and what they did was not thought of as dancing but as tumbling. Real dancing was a ceremonial activity. This was explicit in the Renaissance throughout Western Europe, and implicit right into the 18th century with French Court dancing and ballet; but it disappeared with the Romantic Revolution, and the split at that time between social and spectacular dancing. Faint traces of it can still be detected today in a few of our classical ballets.

At the mechanical level Estampies showed a development from both forms of Carole. Farandole had given us Figures but had made no specific rhythmic patterns; Branles had given us simple rhythms but had limited us to moving in a circle or an arc of a circle. Estampies combined the simple rhythms with a few rudimentary Figures. These were probably no more than movements forwards and backwards, going from side to side, and changing places by the partners. Their importance lies in their combination with a specific rhythm and the fact of their orientation. They form a significant floor-track. The Figures in Farandole though far more elaborate, are not thought of as floor-tracks but as patterns made by the line of dancers in relation to itself, not to any external factor.

But the emergence of Estampies was not all gain for our Western culture. When the American psychologist Erich Fromm talks about 'the breaking of the primary bonds' he is deploring our modern failure to respond rhythmically and spontaneously to our fellow human-beings. That we do so fail today is unarguable. Watch a rush-hour crowd getting on or off a London tube-train. See how indifferent they are to each other, how inefficient and inelegant, how uneconomical of their own and other people's muscle work. When dancing Carole we must have had a communal consciousness right along the line, a common flow of force, and a spontaneous response to minimal stimuli. Between then and now there seems to have been a long slow process eroding this old ability. Perhaps with Estampie we can see the first small step on to this downward slope.

Late Mediaeval France

It is hard for us to contemplate the social system of earlier ages with equanimity. Moral outrage is a common reaction to the inequalities that used to be taken for granted. We often find it as embarrassing to mention class today as our grandmothers did to mention sex.

This attitude will not, however, help us to understand our forefathers. Those times are past and nothing we do in the present can alter what then took place. If it is any comfort to us we can remind ourselves that even the greatest aristocrats led lives of a physical rigour that few of us now would survive.

Let us admit that there was a class system, though this was not always so rigid as we imagine. There was a fair amount of flexibility, particularly in England where the nobility was never a closed caste. But by and large society in any country was like a pyramid with the king at the top and a large peasant population constituting the base. (The word peasant is here used technically, not in the pejorative sense which is fashionable at the moment.) Between the two extremes were the nobility, the gentry, the yeomanry, the urban middle classes, and the artisans.

Outside this social continuum, and truly outcast, particularly in the eyes of the Church, were the small number of people who subsequently became our professional dancers. All through the Middle Ages and until the end of the 16th century they were wandering jugglers, tumblers, and buffoons, probably at their least comfortless when they secured a niche in a noble household as a domestic fool. They pose a baffling problem to our modern sensibility; it is an interesting point that the playing of them defeats all our present actors and stage directors.

In the old days everybody danced Carole indiscriminately. It was only with the emergence of Estampie in Provence that we get what we now call 'Court Dancing', a different actual dance form used by the nobility, and later the gentry, but not by the peasantry. Carole persisted of course, and was still danced by everyone, even, they imagined, by the angels in Heaven, and most riotously by Breughel's peasants. At Court level, during the 16th century, Farandole turned into the early form of Coranto, and was subsequently lost in the later development of this dance. Branles lasted at the French court right into the 18th century, though their technique had changed during the 17th. At folk level both these dances continued more or less in the original form, and can still be found in Europe today.

From now on we get a polarization of styles to the tip and to the base of our social pyramid – Court dancing and Folk dancing. But between the lower levels

Top: *The Last Judgement* (detail) by Fra Angelico.
The figure of Threading the Needle in a Farandole, showing the delightful Mediaeval idea of how the angels danced with the 'blessed' in Heaven.

Flemish Fair (detail) by Peter Breughel the Younger.
The other end of the social scale from the angels; romping through a Farandole on the original 'labyrinthine track'.

of the former and the upper levels of the latter there was no distinct division, as there was between any of our dances and the carryings-on of the professional tumblers. In fact there was a fair amount of ground common to both Court and Folk dance, an overlap, and much mutual fertilization.

It was among the dance forms at Court level that any real development took place and so, in spite of the 'Popular' in our title, it is here we must trace our history, at least until the end of the 18th century. Then we can resort again to what would be generally deemed popular.

The first Court dance of which, unlike Estampie, we know enough to make a reconstruction was the great late Mediaeval dance, Basse dance.

Basse dance is interesting because it comes down to us in two quite different forms, the French processional Basse Danse, and the Italian Bassa Danza which at its most characteristic is a Danse à Deux. There is a trend nowadays among some of our younger historians to belittle the Italian Renaissance, to deny that there was a 'waning of the Middle Ages', and to assert that the culture of 15th-century France and Burgundy was every bit a match for that of 15th-century Florence. I long to persuade them to learn and perform the two versions of Basse Dance. I know nothing which so clearly demonstrates the difference between a Mediaeval and a Renaissance mind.

⁂ French Basse Danse is a processional form which, as we have already said, means a number of couples one behind the other, progressing round the circumference of the dancing-floor. The music is usually in triple time, and in regular French Basse Danses it is always in four-bar phrases, called Quaternions or Tetradions. One can think of a Quaternion as 4 bars of 3/4 time, or one bar of very slow 12/8.

The dance has only four available steps, in the ordering of which very strict rules apply. They are recorded by the initial letter of their names. This is a useful form of shorthand which has tempted some enthusiasts to claim it is our first dance notation. The essence of a movement notation, however, is the absence of verbalization, and as in Basse Danse we rely on the *names* of the steps this claim will not hold water.

The steps each take one Quaternion of the music. They are:

1 Two Simples or Singles ss
We met the Simple in Branle Simple and know that it is half the length of a Double. In regular French Basse Danse Simples always come in pairs.

2 Double d
Here is our old friend from Branle Double and Branle Simple.

3 Reprise r
This is a slow backward step taken on a bent knee with the right leg; the body gives almost a slight bow and the left foot is drawn back slowly through 3 counts to close beside the right foot on the 4th.
(When more than one Double or Reprise is done, the second one uses the opposite foot, and so on with alternating feet.)

4 Branle b
(Yes, of course Branle was the name of a dance, but here it means a step. The

student has to keep a wary eye for differing meanings when names appear in different contexts.) Branle is quite an elaborate step compared with Simples, Doubles, and Reprises. Let us describe it for the man and divide our Quaternion into 12 counts, 1.2.3., 4.5.6., 7.8.9., 10.11.12., instead of the usual 4 beats.

The man makes a preliminary rise on the balls of both feet, on the anacrusis, the last count of the preceding Quaternion. Then he:

1 Comes down on the L. heel, bending his R. knee and leaving his R. heel up.
3 Rises on both feet.
4 Comes down on both heels together.
6 Rises on both feet again, and repeats exactly, with the same foot, the movements he made on 1, 3 and 4 on the counts 7, 9 and 10.

There are a head turn and an arm movement to add to this. The head turns outwards on count 1, forward on 4, inwards towards his partner on 7, and forward again on 10. Do not tilt the head at all, but let it move freely and easily on an upright neck.

The man's right hand is holding the girl's left one in a simple low hand-hold (nothing fancy here); they raise their straight (but not stiff) arms slightly forward on 1, back to normal on 4, and repeat this forward and backward movement on 7 and 10.

The girl's foot and hand movements are the same as the man's but she uses the opposite foot and turns her head in the opposite direction. This is one of the few occasions before the late 17th century when partners use opposite feet. Usually they both dance with the same foot, right up to and including the advent of Minuet.

This quite elaborate little step, French Basse Danse Branle, is a stylization of the two minor bows, taken one to the left and one to the right, which often follow the opening Reverence at the beginning of a dance and precede the final Reverence at the end. They are 'lateral movements of courtesy'.

The rules about the sequence of the steps in French Basse Danse are very niggling. The dance consists of a series of 'Measures', which will be of uneven length. In each Measure of a regular Basse Danse the steps must always be in the order of Simples, then Doubles, Reprises and finally Branle. There must be an even number of Simples, an odd number of Doubles (one to five), and an odd number of Reprises (one to five). The number of Doubles and Reprises in any Measure need not be the same.

The simplest and shortest French Basse Danse we know is La Dame. This is what it looks like on paper.

```
R   ss   ddd   rrr   b
    ss   d     r     b
    ss   ddd   r b
                  c
```

The capital R stands for Reverence and the c for 'congé', taking one's leave.

There are literally dozens of French Basse Danses that have come down to us, all slightly different, many of them irregular. Arbeau in his Orchesography (1588) gives us four, but the form would have been old-fashioned by that date.

Les Très Riches Heures du Duc de Berry (April) by Pol de Limbourg.
Of course, no one ever looked exactly like this, but it is how they pictured themselves. The lack of perspective and the high degree of surface decoration are typical of the late Mediaeval French mind and the world of allegory that it inhabited. (c.f. Tobias and the Angel, p. 28.)

What is interesting, however, is that in Arbeau's day they were dancing Basse Danse to the melody of the music which is plainly audible.

Musicologists hold that in earlier times the air of a Basse Danse was stretched out into long notes, each the length of a Quaternion, and put down into the tenor. They are then covered with a great deal of drumming and extra notes in the top parts, utterly obscuring the tune from the non-specialist or non-concentrating ear. The resulting auditory cryptogram delights the musicologist; it represents what as a rule fascinates him most and, copied in black and scarlet manuscript, it gives great visual pleasure. But how anyone ever wanted to dance to it defeats me. It is the only dance I ever have to 'count' to. I am willing to concede that this style may be right for French and Burgundian dancing. But I think that the music for Italian Bassa Danza must have been differently arranged. ✳

In fact I think the whole of French Basse Danse is a tedious affair, guaranteed to strengthen the distaste of those like the late Henry Ford who hold that 'History is Bunk'. It shows the Mediaeval mind at its worst: a lot of finicking little rules within a rigid frame-work. For the release from all these constrictions we must look south to Tuscany where, with Florence in the lead, the springing Renaissance spirit is about to restore to us the freedom of the classical world.

Early Renaissance Italy

The scene: Walmington-on-Sea. The inimitable Captain Mainwaring and his men of Dad's Army are making plans for a party. 'What,' he asks, 'is the first essential for a dance?' 'A floor,' replies Private Pike, and is met with the inevitable 'Stupid boy'.

But Private Pike on this occasion was not being stupid. A floor, in the sense of a level surface, *is* the first essential for human dancing; and the shape, the size, and the surface of the dancing floor are all important factors in the ultimate form and style of dance that emerges at any particular period.

A great deal of Mediaeval life was spent out of doors in the summer and Carole, particularly Farandole, was suited to outdoor performances, for it could be danced even among trees. The dancers would be used to moving over turf. When winter drove them indoors and the castle hall was the scene of Christmas revels, the dancing surface would not be very different from the outdoor one, for the stone floor would be covered with rushes. These would give a spongy feel to the foot.

This was so at least in France and the Low Countries, in Burgundy and the Holy Roman Empire. But Italy was different. Here we tended to get elegantly proportioned palace rooms as opposed to castle halls, and underfoot, instead of rushes, beautiful marble floors.

On a floor surface such as this, much more control of the foot is possible, and in Northern Italy in the 1400s as an important factor of the technique, we begin to get a rise and fall of the body from the insteps. It is one of the two basic technical features, the other being a contrary movement of the shoulders and torso against the forward foot and leg. This is an extension of our normal opposition movement when we walk, swinging the right arm forward to balance us as we step out with our left foot.

✳ This latter, the contrary movement, is called Maniera. It has the same root as the word 'Mannerism' which our art historians today use as a descriptive term for the period of Italian art following the Renaissance and preceding Baroque. It is a flowing movement comparable with good épaulement in ballet (épaulement means having the shoulders at an angle, not square to the front), and identical with the 'Contra-body movement' of English Modern Ballroom dancing.

The opposition movement of our shoulders must always have been natural to Western dancing because of the linked arms in Carole, particularly in Farandole.

Imagine a file of dancers all facing forward. The leader puts his right hand back and takes the left hand of the girl behind him; she puts her right hand back and takes the left hand of the man behind her, and so on down the line. They will all now be standing with their left shoulders slightly forward and their right shoulders slightly back, instead of having their shoulders square to the front. If they now step forward with their left foot they will be in what we call an 'open' position of the body; the left leg and left arm are forward, the right leg and right arm are back. This is the position of bodies on many classical friezes. But on our second step, when we put our right foot forward we are in a 'crossed' position; an imaginary line from the right shoulder down the right leg makes a X with the line from the left shoulder down the left leg. This is a true contra-body position and it will occur on every other step of a Farandole walk. On the alternate steps

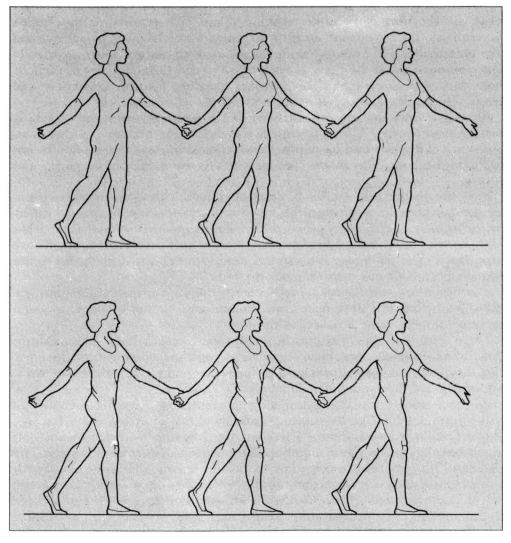

Top: The 'open' position.   Bottom: The 'crossed' position.

the bodies will be in the 'open' position. What is obvious is that they were rarely in Farandole in the position we call 'en face', that is with our shoulders at right angles to our line of progression.

The quality of resilience in the rise and fall of the body was called Aiere. Its meaning was not limited just to the rise and sink on the instep, but extended to the springing steps as well. So it is really the same as 'Balon' in ballet today – the quality of natural rebound from the landing or sinking.

This rise and fall of the body whether just on the instep or actually springing off the ground ('relevé', 'sauté', respectively in ballet), was fundamental in old Western dancing. So important in fact that we actually called it 'the Movement'. This is a technical term and, as you can imagine, confuses many research students who naturally think it means any sort of movement. The 'Movimento' meant one rise and fall, usually accompanied by Maniera, the shoulder movement. By the time of Baroque technique (late 17th century to the French Revolution), 'the Movement' meant a preliminary sink followed by one rise and fall. This disappeared from technique during the 19th century, when we tried to dance on our toes all the time. It re-emerged in the 1920s in three of the four main dances of English Modern Ballroom dancing, Foxtrot, Quickstep, and Waltz. The fourth, Tango, has no rise and fall. ✲

All this is only the mechanical basis of the great achievement of Italian Renaissance dancing. The achievement was due to the brilliance of one man, Domenico of Ferrara, and his pupils, the chief of whom was Guglielmo l'Hebreo (William the Jew). The dances they have left us are models of simplicity and beauty.

They are divided into two kinds, danze and balli. This is the first time a distinction has been made between these two words. It does not denote any difference of technique, as so many people think today; nor does it mean that there is a mime element in the balli. There most certainly is not; both danze and balli are pure dance. The difference is a musical one: a danza has a uniform rhythm throughout; a ballo has more than one rhythm.

(Art historians, when speaking of the early Italian Renaissance, employ the term Quattrocento. This is merely an Italian word for the 1400s. It is useful because it implies the style as well as the date.)

There were four main rhythms in use in Quattrocento Italy: Bassa Danza, Quadinaria, Salterello, and Piva. Basse Danza was the slowest and stateliest and Piva the quickest and most peasant-like. Balli must contain at least two of them, but usually had three, and often all four.

It is interesting to note that four main, and contrasting, rhythms seem often to be the norm. In the High Renaissance in England and France we have Pavane, Galliard, Almain and Coranto. These last two, together with Sarabande and Gigue make up the four basic numbers of the Baroque Instrumental Suite. The 18th and 19th centuries are exceptions to this rule of four: the 18th century with its plethora of dance rhythms, and the 19th with its poverty – really only waltz can be taken seriously. Then in English Modern Ballroom we get quadruple rhythms again, Foxtrot, Quickstep, Waltz, and Tango. When all four of these are used in one dance, as they often are in Formation dancing, we have something directly comparable with a Quattrocento ballo.

One of the interesting things about these Italian dances is their liking for file formation, i.e. the dancers in a line, but behind each other, not side-by-side. What is obvious here is the influence of Farandole, the forward-moving version of Carole, and the one popular in southern countries, as opposed to Branles, the sideways-moving ones, so typical of France. This formation looks beautiful and natural in balli like Jupiter and Vercepe, which have a file for three and for five respectively, but in Basse Dances like Alexandresca and Ginevra, where there is only one couple, it does strike some modern eyes as a little odd. Especially as the girl is standing *behind* the man. This would have been her natural place in the Farandole line of course, with a man always leading. One has on occasion to remind more radical students that there was no Women's Lib. in the Renaissance. Besides, Courtly Love, with its adoration of the Lady, never had as strong a hold in Italy as it had in France, where in all the dances we have found the woman is always *beside* the man. The Italian file position calls to mind Robert Browning's poem, 'My Last Duchess', which gives a brilliant impression of the mind of a Renaissance prince.

But if file formation seems attractive and unusual it presents great difficulties in staging. All these Italian dances require the proportions and area of one of their own palazzo rooms, usually very long in relation to its width (though that was not inconsiderable). In London the only adequate places I know would be St. John's, Smith Square, Inigo Jones's Banqueting House in Whitehall, and Cecil Sharp House, the Headquarters of the English Folk Dance and Song Society, and they would be suitable only if we left no space for a modern audience! On a normal stage we would be half-way up the stalls by the end of the dance, unless we regularly 'cooked' all the figures, working up stage wherever possible.

'Cooking' would be most reprehensible, for it would ruin the exquisite spatial design which is half the beauty of all Domenico's dances (the other half being the subtlety of the apparently simple rhythm). Domenico enunciated three qualities which he considered essential for a good dance.
1 Misura.
2 Memoria.
3 Compartimento di terreno.

1 *Misura*
This means 'proportion' and was a fundamental concept of Renaissance thought.

2 *Memoria*
This is, of course, memory in our usual sense of remembering the sequence of steps and the floor-tracks, but it is very much more. It is the conception of a dance as a whole, as that single unique experience which constitutes a work of art. This is something very different from the long enchaînement of steps which today so often seems to pass as 'choreography'.

3 *Compartimento di terreno*
The late Mrs Dolmetsch translated this as 'the apportionment of one's terrain' and I cannot hope to better that. It is a quality badly neglected in professional

training today; but then it is not much needed on large stages and in television studios, where spatial niceties are either lost or distorted by the camera. This third essential of Domenico means the apparently spontaneous ability to make one's range of movement fit exactly and harmoniously into the available space, leaving both the dancer and the audience with a feeling of effortless ease and grace, of something which in this chaotic world is blissfully right.

One sees this happen sometimes at a Highland ball when a few very good men find themselves in the same set, and most notably, always and everywhere, with the unique Astaire.

※ In contrast with all this mathematical and aesthetic theory, the steps themselves were still very simple, or appeared to be so. They are our old friends Simples and Doubles, though now they have to be taken with Aiere and Maniera, that is with a rise and fall and with contrary movement. To take a normal closed Simple with the left foot you must, before you even begin to move, press on the ground with your right foot; then, *taking your weight forward with you,* you advance your left foot and put the ball of it down gently, not letting yourself go high up on the toes like a three-quarter point in Ballet. During this advance the pressure and momentum from the ball of the back foot must be maintained, until the weight is transferred on to the forward foot. Then you release the back foot and unhurriedly bring it level with the front one, when you sink down slowly through both insteps. The step bears no resemblance to a posé* in Ballet today except in its gross mechanics: i.e. that it consists of one weight change with a progression forward.

Maniera is achieved in the Simple by bringing the right shoulder and the right side of the torso forward in opposition to the advancing left leg. Then as the weight is transferred forward the shoulders even out and finish straight to the front as the body lowers from the rise. There is no hard pushing movement in Maniera; it is almost a swing of the shoulders, but not quite. When one is doing two Simples, a left and a right, the shoulder movement feels almost as if it were a figure of eight. But Maniera must never look forced or exaggerated.

To do a normal Double starting with the left foot we begin exactly as if we were going to make a Simple: press on the ball of the right foot, pushing the body upwards and forwards. Take the first step on the ball of the left foot but do not sink. Keep up while you place the right foot forward on the ball, and the left foot forward again on the ball. Only then complete the step with a slow controlled sink through both feet as in the Simple. Because the rhythm is Quick, Quick, Slow and you think you are 'on your toes', do not take cramped little steps: this is a great mistake.

The Maniera in a Double is: oppose the front foot on the first step and use the whole duration of the step to level out the shoulders again. Never try to make three oppositions in a Double, for you would look absurd.

Tobias and the Angel by a follower of Verrocchio.
Not a fully naturalistic presentation but compared with the French Miniature (page 23) almost photographic. The sense of bodies inhabiting actual space, the depth, the weight and the movement all express the Renaissance mind. Both figures show 'Maniera', the Angel in a contrary position, and Tobias in an open one.

The Reprise, the slow backward step in French Basse Danse, is often taken to the side in Italian work. A particularly characteristic sideways Reprise is when the body makes a half-turn to face the opposite direction: the right leg steps *across* the left leg, and one begins to turn to the left; as one puts the ball of the right foot down one swivels, momentarily only, on the balls of both feet, before transferring the weight fully on to the ball of the right and completing 180° of turn. Then one unhurriedly closes the left foot to the right and slowly sinks. In Bassa Danza this step has the same timing as a French Reprise: if we are counting 4 to the Quaternion ♩ ♩ ♩ | ♩ ♩ ♩ | ♩ ♩ ♩ | ♩. ‖ , then the first step comes on the first beat of the first bar and the closing of the foot is not until the fourth bar, taking this whole note to bring one's heels to the ground. In the Italian step one has risen and is on the balls of the feet for the three slow counts before the close, a very different matter from the easy drag-back of the foot on the flat in the French version.

The most popular way of making a full turn in this Italian technique is called a Volta Tonda. It consists of two Simples and the turning Reprise we have just described. If we are turning to the left then the first Simple is made with the right foot, putting it across in front of the left leg, and turning 90° on it. In stage terms we are now facing the Prompt side, the audience's right-hand side, having started facing down-stage. We make the second Simple with the left foot, turning a further 90° to face up-stage, and finally the turning Reprise as we have described it above. This completes a 360° turn and we finish facing down-stage as we started.

It will be noted that the turn on the first Simple and the Reprise is what in Ballet today would be called 'en dedans' as opposed to 'en dehors'; 'en dedans' means turning towards the inside of the moving leg, i.e. towards the big-toe side of it, as opposed to 'en dehors', which is turning outwards towards the little-toe side.

A Volta Tonda takes two Quaternions of Basse Dance music,

♩ ♩ ♩ | ♩ ♩ ♩ | ♩ ♩ ♩ | ♩. ‖ ♩ ♩ ♩ | ♩ ♩ ♩ | ♩ ♩ ♩ | ♩. ‖

If we are playing at 10 Quaternions to the minute, a very moderate speed, then each Quaternion will take 6 seconds. This means that we have to balance on the ball of one foot – with apparently no consciousness of difficulty, unlike the ballerina in the Rose Adagio* – for $4\frac{1}{2}$ seconds. ❊

It is the necessity for seemingly effortless control through long sustained movements that makes it almost impossible today to get Domenico's dances adequately demonstrated. They require a combination of body skills that we simply do not develop.

1 A firm muscular control of the hip girdle. Many people have never tensed the muscles round the pelvis in their lives.

2 A 'pulled-up' knee.
This is when the leg is not just straight in the ordinary sense, but the knee-joint is

'locked' by the contraction of the quadriceps, the big muscle on the front of the thigh.

We can find out what this means by a simple experiment. Put your leg up forwards on the arm of a chair or the edge of a table. See that it is supported comfortably on the back of the heel or the back of the ankle, and let it be quite straight but not strained in any way. Don't choose too high a support if your hamstrings are short. (Our hamstrings are the muscles at the back of our thighs which, when they are tight, prevent our touching our toes without bending our knees.) Now put your fingers on your kneecap and feel that you can move it from side to side; it will wobble quite a lot. This is what happens with most of us when we think our legs are straight. Now put your hand on the front of your thigh and tense the big muscle, the quadriceps. When you've got it firmly contracted, hold the contraction and feel your kneecap again. You will find it is completely fixed.

This is the 'locked', fully-extended knee, which gives us the straight, strong leg we require. With the knee braced like this we are able to transmit a thrust from the foot directly up into the back with no risk of wobble or deflection on the way.

(It is interesting that 'weak-kneed' should be used figuratively in English to mean 'inability to stand firm, want of resolution'.)

Both these first two requirements, the controlled pelvis and the braced knee can be seen today in any well-trained ballet-dancer. It is when we come to the third requirement that even they fail to qualify.

3 The sprung foot.
An elastic strength in the combined ankle and instep which allows us to use our feet as the natural levers and shock-absorbers that they are. This results in a lithe, tiger-like smoothness concealing enormous controlled strength. We hardly ever see this today. Most of our professionals spend their training learning to perform a range of difficult movements, many of an acrobatic type. Their feet take a good deal of punishment. The girls learn to use the foot as a spike, albeit blunted, on which the body can be supported in highly unusual postures. The men, although not working on point, still have to dance on a high, uneconomical $\frac{3}{4}$ point, which often produces a rigid foot, and always deprives the body of much of its natural resilience.

It is almost unthinkable, by today's standards, that they should spend sorely-needed time and energy achieving an apparently simple way of moving which is right outside their present range, and well outside the grasp of most modern choreographers. Amateur dancers, on the other hand, who sometimes have very neat footwork, hardly ever have the necessary torso and leg strength to sustain the slow tempi of this technique. It's yet another instance of 'never the time and the place and the loved one all together'.

As for the general public, the sagging deportment which has been fashionable for the last couple of decades may be, let us hope, only temporary. But for the last two centuries, even when good posture was admired, our centre of gravity has gone back appreciably from its Renaissance position. Our poise has altered fundamentally and to have one's weight back over the heels is commonplace today. One cannot hope to perform any pre-19th-century dance technique unless one's centre of gravity is brought dead over the middle of the arch of the instep with every single weight change. This means getting it several inches farther forward than is natural today.

A constant question about early dancing is 'What did they do with their arms?' This is a tricky one for there are few set arm movements until the later 17th century, and the kind of arm positions seen in Ballet today were *never* used before the 19th century. In Quattrocento Italy the arms must have been particularly fluid and graceful – they simply floated round the body, now and then emphasizing the musical phrase, a little way out from one's sides. This is not very helpful to tell modern pupils, but there is a useful little exercise we can do.

Straighten your arms down by your sides and press the inside of your wrists hard against the outside of your thighs while you count ten slowly. When you release this pressure you will find your arms floating out to each side a little way away from you – perhaps eight or twelve inches. This is the position in which Renaissance people would have carried their arms when dancing, with the elbows well away from their waists and an open, easy look. Then when you employ Maniera (the opposition shoulder movement) the arms will swing under the moving shoulder joints, one forward and one back with the contrary position of the body. Give a slight emphasis to this movement, rather like a flow and an ebb or a very rudimentary figure of eight, and you should be well on the way to good arm work. Look as often as you can at their paintings, particularly Leonardo da Vinci and Botticelli. Resist the temptation to translate them into Modern Dance or Ballet, but try to imagine their own essential movement quality.

And here we face a horrible danger. That is the school of thought that claims passionately that all these dances were 'dramatic'. The answer to this is 'Yes, they were'. But they were dramatic in the sense that German Lieder are dramatic, as opposed to the overt theatricality of operatic arias; i.e. purely within their own musical structure. There was no extraneous emotional expression added to the pure dance form and there was certainly no mime.

Michael Baxandall in his 'Painting and Experience in 15th Century Italy' puts the matter perfectly. (He is talking of paintings but his words are equally true of Domenico's dances.) He says that our ability to understand art of this kind 'depends on our disposition to expect and work for tacit relationships with and within a group of people . . . an art where a pattern of people – not gesticulating or lunging or grimacing – can still stimulate a strong sense of some psychological interplay, is the problem: it is doubtful if we have the right predispositions to see such refined innuendo at all spontaneously.'

In dance drama today we expect the dramatic content of a work to be one of two things: either explicit, as in the mime of Classical Ballet, or exaggeratedly expressionist, as in so many modern dance productions. There are wonderful exceptions of course: one thinks of Anthony Tudor's Jardin au Lilas. But, by and large, our palates have been coarsened to a dangerous degree. Peter Ustinov said of the drama critics, 'they have eaten so much curry, that they can no longer taste asparagus'.

An added awkwardness is the difference in our social background. Domenico's dances were performed by people who, by our standards, were a small, élite group. That they could move with simplicity and sincerity strikes us as odd. In this climate of opinion I hesitate to repeat Domenico's instructions to us of how we should feel and look when we are dancing: they were 'seigneurial and angelic'.

The High Renaissance

England and France in the late 16th and early 17th centuries

By the end of the following century the beauty and simplicity of Italian Quattrocento dancing had disappeared on its home ground. It was hidden under a mass of fussy footwork and rather trumpery music, at least so far as the books of dance instruction and description go. The old flowing spaciousness seemed to be out of favour with the late 16th-century dancing-masters, of whom two, called Caroso and Negri, have left us substantial volumes of their compositions. Some of these, particularly in the steps, seem to be much more like Spanish dancing today. Yet outside the dancing-masters' work the music of Monteverdi brings to mind the movement qualities that the previous century had so admired; so they may have survived after all, but we have no direct evidence in Italy for this.

The countries where at least some of Domenico's virtues now began to make an appearance were Elizabethan England and France. Admittedly the dances had shed much of their Italianate subtlety, particularly rhythmic subtlety, and the French and English sense of space was not yet so highly developed. This was to come later, when the floor patterns of Baroque* technique were to rival anything we had seen before. But their dancing at its best does seem to have had a noble simplicity that would have earned the old Maestro's approval.

The chief dances were the four we have mentioned already, Pavane, Galliard, Almain, and Coranto. To these must be added Brawls, Measures, Volta, and in England the Old and the New Country Dance. They cover between them the whole range of old dance forms: communal chain dance, processional dance, danse à deux, and figure dance.

Pavane

⌘ Pavane was the great slow rhythm of the High Renaissance,* and incidentally the only example of the main dance rhythm of any age being in duple time, until we come to Foxtrot in our present century. In its unadapted form it is a dance of baffling simplicity. It consists of two Simples, one to the left and one to the right, and a Double forward; two Simples, one to the right and one to the left, and a Double back. This is splendid and suitable for a processional dance, which Pavane often was, but very difficult to sustain in a Danse à Deux. (The couple, as was usual, both used the same foot.) ⌘

Measures

Pavane music was used for two other purposes. In that age it was the accompanying music for all ceremonial activities, state occasions, weddings and funerals. It was also used for a set Figure dance called Measures; this bore the same relation to Pavane as Formation dancing does to ordinary Ballroom dancing today.

'Measures' may mean several other dances too (and the word in its singular, 'measure', has various meanings), but this figure dance was the most likely interpretation at this time; it is the dance that Beatrice, in Shakespeare's Much Ado about Nothing, called 'full of state and ancientry'.

Pavane is often said to come from a root meaning 'peacock' and so we should move like peacocks when dancing it. This is nonsensical advice. First of all the derivation is by no means certain; the name may come from a quite different root. Secondly, even if the derivation were correct we would look absurd strutting like birds in a dance that requires just as much lithe, velvety control as any of Domenico's. One might as well try to imitate a fox in a Foxtrot. Like so much colourful and erroneous advice, this has attracted and misled many people – to the grave detriment of dancing.

Pavane is based rhythmically on Branle Double, and it is possible that Estampie Double was the original of its very simple space pattern.

Galliard

Galliard is a unique dance. In a court entertainment it can be an actual solo for the man, and at any time it is a virtual solo. It is the first time that a dance at noble level (as opposed to a tumbler's performance) has contained enough pattern for one body by itself. All the Danses à Deux hitherto have depended on the two bodies making spatial patterns in relation to each other, but in Galliard the girl's role is spatially negligible. She paces about in no particular pattern admiring the man, and occasionally performing a mild Galliard passage herself to give him time to get his breath and renew his energies. It is the great athletic dance of all time, and it is interesting to note that it died because it became vulgar and an occasion for obvious showing off.

✳ Galliard rhythm comes down to us from Branle Gai, which give us a count of 6; 4 even springs and a pause for 2.

$$\textnormal{♩ ♩ ♩ | ♩. ‖}$$
$$\textnormal{1 2 3 4 (to 6)}$$

We next get Tordion, which is a preliminary to Galliard. Here we still have the 4 springs as in Branle Gai, but for the 2-beat pause we substitute what they called a Cadenza.

To do a Cadenza one stands, let us say, on the right foot with the left foot out in front as if one were about to step on to it; but instead of stepping forward, one jumps off the right foot, and draws back and lands on the left, immediately placing the ball of the right foot down in front. This position is called a Posture Droite.

The whole of Tordion step therefore goes:
Spring on to the left foot; count 1
Spring on to the right foot; count 2
Spring on to the left foot; count 3
Spring on to the right foot; count 4

Your weight is now on your right so bring the left foot forward as if to step on it, but don't; instead perform the Cadenza as described above. The timing I like for this is ♩ ♩ ♩ |♩. ♪♩ ‖. Other timings for the Tordion Cadenza are possible but not, I think, so lively.

Having performed one Tordion step starting with the left foot and finishing in Posture Droite, we must begin the next with the forward right foot of the Posture. This is touching the ground, but it has no weight on it. It is a little tricky for some people who want to put their weight on the forward foot and do every step with the left. This is wrong, however, for Galliard, which was the outcome of Tordion, is the first symmetrical· dance we have. Every step in it which is done with the left foot leading must be repeated with the right. This was something quite new then, though it is a commonplace today.

A regular Galliard passage takes the four springs and Cadenza of Tordion, but substitutes for the four plain forward springs (L.R.L.R.) a variety of jumps, hops, swings, beats, and cuts by the man. Each passage is performed with the left foot leading (6 counts), repeated with the right foot (12 counts), and this 12-count sequence is repeated once to make up a regular Galliard measure of 24 beats. On the repeats the passage can, if suitable, be turned to give variety; make $\frac{1}{4}$ turn on each of the first 4 jumps, and then you will be facing forward again for the Cadenza.

It is possible to make a Galliard passage with a deferred Cadenza. Instead of only 4 springs etc. we make 10, and then do the Cadenza on the counts 11 and 12. This can be repeated only once to make up the regular measure of 24 counts, or 8 bars of $\frac{3}{4}$ time.

It is theoretically possible to do a deferred Cadenza passage of 22 springs and a Cadenza on the counts 23 and 24. This is not really advisable as it would take two whole measures to accommodate the passage with its repeat, and this makes it all a bit lengthy.

The jumps in Galliard are not at all like a Ballet allegro enchaînement*, though they are often demonstrated like this. The leg swings are natural gravity swings, as are the arm movements which oppose the legs. The whole dance is very masculine, but much more subtle than is usually thought. ✠

The English were particularly good at Galliard. It has been suggested that this was so because we regarded it as a sport rather than an art. But that is a libel, for in the last decades of the 16th century the flowering of the arts in England could stand comparison with any country and any age. London was 'a nest of singing birds' and the greatest dramatist the world has ever known was walking in her streets and writing for her playhouse. That remarkable woman Elizabeth Tudor – Gloriana – was on the throne, and we had just defeated the might of Spain and her Armada. We were 'the dancing English'. Galliard was our great dance. It has never been equalled since.

The music of Galliard is poorly understood today and the rhythm and tempo badly misrepresented in most recordings. As we said about Branle Gai, the six counts are not like two bars of waltz time. The first three counts must be equally strong and the fourth very strong indeed. 'God Save the Queen' is in Galliard rhythm, though not in Galliard form of a 24-beat measure (it is irregular). The best Galliard rhythm I have ever heard is the 19th-century aria 'La donna e mobile' from Verdi's Rigoletto. The story goes that Verdi was so frightened that the tune would be pirated that he hid it even from the orchestra, until the very last moment. Not only has it the magnificent dynamics that we need to dance Galliard, but it is usually played and sung at a perfect tempo for it. All very different from many attempted 'authentic' performances.

Volta

The last stage of Branle Gai rhythm, having come down through Tordion and Galliard, was Volta. This is very much a couple dance and is often thought to be the prototype of Waltz. But that is quite wrong. The fourth step and Cadenza of the regular Galliard passage is turned into a lift of the girl, up and round him, by the man. The exact hold that he uses to lift the girl has never been settled. The one we see in the paintings would give insufficient purchase (ref. p. 6 and 7).

Volta was a scandalous dance as were, later on, the Charleston and the Black Bottom. They are all equally unimportant in the development of our dance history, for they represent dead ends, but they each made a great furore in their time. Volta is one of the few old dances every theatrical producer has heard of and wants. Arbeau castigates it severely as he says you may catch sight of the girl's bare knees. (In those days their stockings were gartered and ended below the knee.) In view of the structure of the farthingale there was a risk of seeing a good deal more than that and, as the girls wore no pants, a real danger of un-seemliness.

But the vulgarity of Volta does not depend on its salaciousness, but on its lack of structural and spatial interest, and compared with Galliard, its rhythmic banality.

Almain (Alman, Almayne, Allemande, almost any spelling)

Almain is the most peasant-like of the four main dances. The name just means the 'German' dance. It is duple time, and has a characteristic Double of its own. This consists of three steps, L.R.L., and a hop on the left foot bringing the right knee up at right angles. The double is rhythmically the same as Branle de Bourgogne, often called the fourth Brawl. This consists of Doubles with three steps and a hop.

It is a processional dance, and has an unusual hand-hold which adds to the folky effect. In Pavane and other great dances the man holds the girl's hand very simply and *low down*. There are only two exceptions to that rule. One was in Domenico's technique where you can get a strange hold of the little fingers, with the arm bent and close in against the shoulder. The other is in Almain. Here the man bends his right arm at the elbow, presenting his forearm horizontally to the girl, with the palm of the hand facing down. She places her left forearm along the top of his right one, letting it rest easily there.

This peculiar arm-hold together with the rather clumping Double gives Almain a character all of its own. I always tell pupils to imagine they are Flemish burghers when they are dancing it. Almain usually opens with at least four Doubles, and then the couples each do some simple little figure, and off we go again with the Almain Doubles. It was in great use in the 'commonings' or

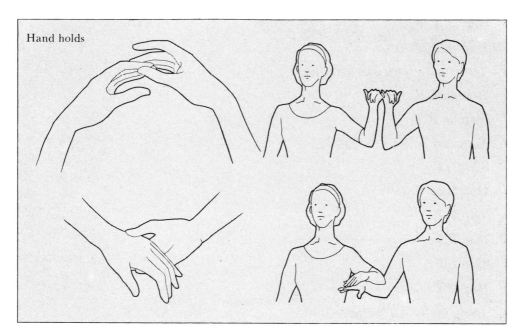

Top: Fairy tale pantomime.
Bottom: Simple authentic.

Top: Domenico.
Bottom: Almain.

'communings' which were the dances after a masque at court, when the masquers and their former audience joined up and danced together.

One very real problem with Almain is the tempo. In any dance that contains a jumping step (here the hop) there is a limit to the slowness at which the music can be played. Nearly all musicians feel that Almain music should be played more slowly than this limit, or at least that *some* Almain music should. In this one instance I sympathize with them and feel that here we have a problem which we have not yet solved.

Coranto

All the dances so far listed in this chapter have had their roots in an old Branle rhythm, but Coranto is an exception; it developed from Farandole.

In the late Middle Ages when we lost the 'arched' figures from Farandole we were left with the Hey and the labyrinthine track. The regular walking, running, or skipping steps began to be thought insufficiently interesting when travelling along this random track, and various combinations of hops and skips and jumps began to be done. But none of these was sacrosanct in the way Galliard rhythm was, rooted deeply in Branle Gai.

The evidence of Coranto step is highly confusing and no two people agree about it, but the solution I like best is the following. It takes 4 bars of 6/8 time to the rhythm

♩ ♪♩. | ♩ ♪♩. | ♩ ♪♩ ♪|♩ ♪♩. ‖

♩ Hop on R.F.

♪ Step on L.F.

♩. Jump on to both feet together.

♩ Hop on L.F.

♪ Step on R.F.

♩. Jump on both feet together.

♩ Step L.F.

♪ Hop L.F.

♩ Step R.F.

♪ Hop R.F.

♩ Step L.F.

♪ Hop R.F.

♩. Jump on both feet together.

If the second half is syncopated it is even livelier and much more interesting. ✳

The jumps should be not so much up and high, but along the ground. Their clear springing steps seem to echo the lively and witty imagination of the Elizabethan mind. Shakespeare in his Henry V talks of 'swift corantos'.

Branles

Apart from mentioning the high head-dresses of the late Middle Ages we have said very little so far about the clothes. There was a big change from the costumes of Quattrocento Italy to those of Tudor England. The men's short velvet tunics and the girls' soft silk dresses gave a great freedom and flow to Domenico's technique. When we come to the late Elizabethan age we see the human body as positively upholstered. The women were far the worse sufferers with their farthingales, those great hooped underskirts, and their long-waisted boned bodices and often monstrous sleeves. But the men were fairly well buckram'd and brocaded too. Ruffs, jewels, lace and embroidery encrusted on to everything added the final note.

What this built-up, built-out costume did affect was the amount of Maniera, the Contra-body movement, they were able to employ. This was now much more constrained, but we must beware of thinking that they ever danced woodenly because our modern demonstrators, when attired like this, do so. ✳ What did alter, though, was the old oblique way of doing the Doubles and Simples in a Brawl. In the Middle Ages we had simply walked to one side and the other with our feet at an oblique angle to our line of progression, and our shoulders equally oblique. Now in Branles Double and Simple we all turn to face the centre of our circle, or arc of a circle, with our feet, parallel to each other, pointing into the middle where we are facing. Then we make our steps directly to the side. A Double goes like this:

1 Step on L.F. to the left, on the ball of the foot.
2 Bring the R.F. up near to the L.F. but do not close it tightly, with both feet still on toes.
3 Step on the L.F. again out to the left, still on toes.
4 Close the R.F. to the L.F. and sink slowly on to the heels.
Repeat to the right, leading with the right foot.

A Simple is just one step to the side on the ball of the foot, and a close with the other foot and sink.

In Branle Gai and Branle de Bourgogne we still have to turn obliquely. ✳

The old and new Country Dance

(This applies to England, not to France. In France the Folk dances at this time were nearly all Branles.)

To trace the true development of Folk dance in England would take a body of historical anthropologists working for a long time. What we can state for certain is that most of our 'English Country Dances' were not 'Folk' dances at all. This is not to say that they were not danced by country people, and in a rustic style; but they were also danced by monarchs, and the nobility and gentry in a courtly style. They were to continue to be so danced for the next two hundred years.

There are two great exceptions which are ritual folk dances, and are unique in European culture – Morris and Sword Dance. (These will be treated separately in the chapter entitled 'The People's Dances'.)

The printed collections of 'Country Dances' do contain some other true Folk dances, based on ancient Rounds and Heys. A dance called 'Sellenger's Round' in a large circle, is a classic Ring Dance and obviously very old. 'Dargason' a dance in a straight line, is based on a linear Hey, in fact you can see the two Farandole lines meeting in it; it opens with movements called 'siding' and 'arming' which may have been added at a later date. Elegant little squares for four, and the other square and long dances come from another source. Melusine Wood considered that they came from comparable models among Domenico's Balli. The old country dance for four, named after a dancing-master, 'Parson's Farewell', has distinct resemblances to the ballo Anello, and other correspondences can be traced.

The 'Country' in 'Country Dance' may in fact not have meant 'rural' originally, but may have come from 'contra' or 'contre'. This would denote the couple facing each other across a set, as opposed to facing the Presence as they did in the more stately forms of the Danse à Deux, or in those Balli which were danced not in closed sets but in files or rows. Now the Balli that were composed for closed sets (e.g. Anello, Gelosia) were less grand, and presumably therefore more informal, than the 'open' dances. This would help the confusion of 'contra' with 'rustic' and in the conflation produced a tangle of meaning difficult to unravel. I find this explanation not just plausible, but likely.

Whatever its source the English Country Dance is a very important dance form. It is one of our two contributions as a nation to European choreography, the other being English Modern Ballroom dancing. (Although we were so good at Galliard, we can make no claims to be its originators – its source was unarguably a French Branle.) In the years that loom ahead after Gloriana's sun had set our English Country Dances were to be the only successful rebels against an enormous French tyranny and in the end they were to see its utter defeat and extinction.

The background of belief

Most of us today when invited to a dance set out with no more idea in our heads than the pleasant expectation of meeting our friends and enjoying the pleasures of sociability and rhythmic movement to rhythmic music.

Few of us would pause to consider whether next autumn's harvest might be affected by the choice of our right or our left foot when we begin to dance, nor whether our progression round the dance-floor, clockwise or anti-clockwise, might help or hinder the stars in their courses. Such notions would strike most of us as very far-fetched.

So we find it hard at first to identify with Mediaeval men, who did believe just such things. I remember the shocked horror of a publisher's reader when I assured him that this was true; he had thought I was pulling his leg. These old beliefs depend on what anthropologists call Sympathetic Magic.

We occasionally see films of primitive people even today jumping up and down on the ground after they have planted the seeds of whatever cereal their tribe subsists on. They believe the energy they are expending in this ritual dance (for it is a dance) will enter into the earth and make the seeds grow bigger and stronger and produce a fine crop for them. That is Sympathetic Magic in its simplest form.

Something comparable with this, though not quite the same, happens to us when we see a man running for a bus. We may stop in our tracks to watch whether he will catch it or not and, just as he makes a final effort to jump on the platform, we find ourselves tensing our own muscles as if to help him! It can be argued that this is pure empathy, the result on our nervous system of seeing the man's muscular strain, but I think at some level of our consciousness or subconsciousness we feel that we are really helping him.

This was what Mediaeval man believed too: that by adding his energies in a compatible way to the forces of Nature he was helping the benevolent forces and hindering the malevolent ones.

To understand what he meant by 'compatible' we have to acquaint ourselves with his way of looking at the world. He believed in what is called a 'Geocentric Cosmology'. This simply means a picture of the universe with our world in the middle of it, and the sun travelling round us. Before Copernicus's 'revolutionary' ideas were accepted this was the common belief.

Round our globe as their centre, moved seven concentric spheres in which were the planets. The moon was the inmost of these, and the word 'sublunary' has a technical meaning: it denotes the area within the moon's orbit in contrast with the outer space beyond it. The middle one of the seven encircling planets was the sun. To people to whom a bad harvest was a disaster, and two successive bad harvests meant death for many, the sun was the great life-giving force. Everything must be done to help him in his work of ripening their corn and producing fodder for their farm animals.

In the old chain dance they therefore always moved first to the left, or clock-

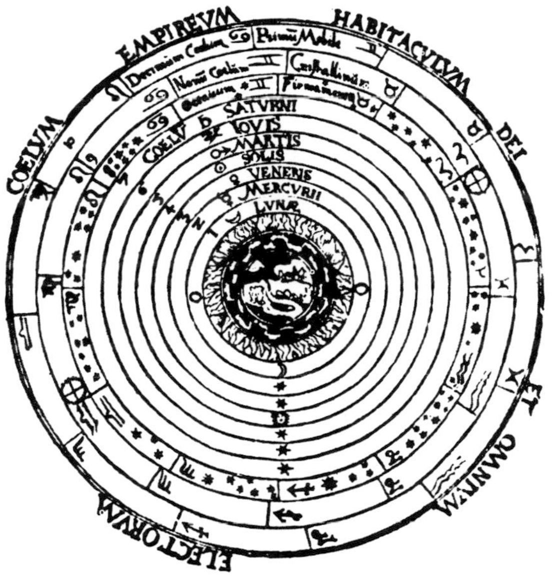

The Universe according to Peter Apian (1533).

wise, the way they thought the sun travelled from east to west. This necessitated beginning with the left foot, and as a result all dances begin with the left foot right up to Minuet in the 1670s. To us who live in a right-footed age this sometimes seems awkward, and that both partners in a couple dance should use the same foot, instead of 'mirror' feet, seems very odd. But when one gets one's eye accustomed to such things, it is our modern standards that look wrong in this context.

Besides we have not utterly departed from the old left-footed, clockwise beliefs even today. Our armies still march 'left-right, left-right, left . . ., left . . .', and though formal dinner parties are not to many of us a regular part of our lives, when they do occur the port is still passed clockwise. As late as the 1930s I met dancers in the Highlands who were horrified at the thought of retracing their steps to the right in the opening figure of an eightsome reel; they insisted on taking the entire first phrase right round the circle to the left.

This 'going round the wrong way' is called 'widdershins'. It is reputedly how the witches danced in their covens, calling up the forces of evil when they met at their nocturnal 'Sabbaths'. One can still find country people who would never walk round a church yard except in a clockwise direction. All this may strike many of us today as the unfortunate ignorance and superstition of unenlightened people, 'the bogy-haunted Mediaeval mind', but does in a way tie up with the mental outlook which was being shared by some of the greatest men, and the greatest minds, in the whole history of the West. This is the Platonic view of the nature of reality.

⌘ Plato was one of the two great philosophers of Classical Greece, the other being Aristotle. They are sometimes held to represent the two poles of the human temperament: Aristotle being the scientific, and Plato being the poetical one. But this is a stupid oversimplification. It is very important to understand that no ancient Greek, let alone Plato, ever went around thinking he was living in a wishy-washy sort of dream-world that didn't really mean anything to him. It was because the world of the senses was *already* so vivid and luminous to him that Plato tried to see and think beyond it. It was because ancient Athens was so exquisitely beautiful that he thought that somehow, somewhere there must be beauty which did not decay and die. This was not just somewhere else in the sense of a place, a location. What he said was that outside space and time, not perceivable by our eyes, our ears, or our other senses, there existed, unchanging and unchangeable, the eternal ideas. These ideas are the prototypes and models of everything we experience in our lives on earth. The objects we know through our senses are all participating in these eternal ideas, but the ideas themselves we can 'know' only in our minds. Beyond all the other ideas or forms is 'the form of the good'. This is the key to the whole conception for it is the idea of the good that makes the world intelligible and ourselves intelligent.

Now it is very difficult for human beings to conceive of a world outside space and time, and so this came to be thought of as a real place. We have already said that the word 'sublunary' meant all the area within and beneath the orbit of the moon, i.e. our earth and the air around it. This is the world we know; in which there is change and decay, grief and sorrow, all the ills that flesh is heir to, and ultimately death. Beyond the paths of the moon, where aether takes the place of air, there exists this eternal and changeless world of Plato's thought. No grief, no sorrow, no decay, and no death. Here the stars sing in their courses in perfect tune and perfect harmony.

Which brings us to the second great figure behind this Renaissance picture of our universe. That was Pythagoras, who was a Greek mathematician in the sixth century B.C. It is an amalgam of Platonic-Pythagorean conceptions that constitutes the main stream of Renaissance thought, and particularly their theory about art.

Pythagoras, as every schoolboy knows, is the author of that theorem about the square on the hypotenuse of a right-angled triangle. But he was very much more than that. Probably his greatest achievement was to discover the spatial proportions corresponding to the intervals in our Western musical scales – the octave, the fifth, the fourth and so on.

When a string is vibrated we hear a musical note; but in addition to that main note, we also hear a series of overtones or higher notes. These are caused by secondary vibrations of the string at half its length, at a third, at a quarter, and at even smaller divisions.

The vibrations of the half length string sound the octave above our root note, the triple-division vibrations sound the fifth above that, and the quarter division ones sound the fourth above that again. This last is of course the double octave above the root note. The length of the string is in inverse ratio to the frequency of the vibrations, and the ratios are all simple whole number proportions of $1:2$, $2:3$, and $3:4$.

In the series The Ascent of Man, the late Dr Bronowski explained this with all his usual clarity and infectious enthusiasm. He made it seem fascinating that there should be this close relationship between what we hear and what we see: that the concords in music should be beautiful spatial proportions made audible, and that the harmony, that we see, for instance, in good architecture, should be music made visible. He extended his range of comparisons to include the combination of the elements (e.g. H_2O as water) stressing always the simple whole-number ratios he found all about him.

We can cite the simple ratios of our rhythmic units, the Doubles and Simples, the Anapaests, Dactyls and Spondees. Renaissance man lived in a world in which he saw harmonious proportions everywhere, created by a god who was a mathematician. The object of Art was to harmonize us with the heavenly harmony.

Seen in cold print today this may seem either nonsensical or pretentious. We tend to associate talk of this kind with females in bare feet and chiffon drapes, ambling about a stage or a studio to the strains of Debussy and Ravel in a kind of sub-Isadora haze. All very shaming. But in Elizabethan England these things were believed by the toughest of tough men. Leicester and Sydney, Raleigh and Essex could not conceivably be thought of as 'arty' when they danced. And of course they *did* dance.

It is also the unfortunate fixation in most of our minds that dancing is something done by little girls, or at least by very young women; this prevents our imagining what Elizabeth's Court must have been like. The picture is further confused by the style of late-Victorian and Edwardian operetta and musical comedy. A mixture of German's Merrie England, and Sullivan's The Yeoman of the Guard churns through many people's minds at the very mention of Tudor or Gloriana. Pavane has no place in this scene. Its magnificent simplicity belonged to minds incapable of this colourful shallowness. It is the rhythm that one can feel behind Shakespeare's Tragedies, just as Galliard is the rhythm that comes springing through his Comedies. If our actors could learn to do these dances really well, there would be no need for the extraneous gimmicks that producers introduce into Shakespeare's plays to 'brighten them up'. The total rhythm of each play would then come over as clearly and unarguably as it does in a Mozart opera.

Unity, proportion and clarity, the three necessities for a classical work of art, were present in all the great dances of the Renaissance. It is a world away from the kind of dancing any child today gets the chance to learn or any adult the chance to do. The best introduction to them I know is in the poem called, 'Orchestra' by Sir John Davies (1596). In this he says:

'*Learn them to dance . . .*
And imitate the stars celestial;
For when pale death your vital twist* shall sever,
Your better parts must dance with them forever.' ✖

The French Connection

An age of transition

The Mid-Seventeenth Century – France and England

In one sense every age is an age of transition, where nothing remains completely the same over a period of time, but the 17th century was much more changeable than most. At its beginning we were still not free of the old Mediaeval world and its traditions, by the end there is a good deal that seems fairly modern.

From our point of view, in the world of dancing, the greatest changes took place in the middle decades of the century, probably from about 1620 to 1660 or 1670. They went with the great changes in costume from the stiff, padded brocades of Elizabethan and Jacobean England to the soft silks and satins, the lace and the ribbons, of Charles II and Louis XIV.

Two very odd changes took place that we cannot fully explain. We began to put heels on our shoes. We called them 'high' heels, but they were not high by today's standards. If we had been using the shoes for dancing the heels would not have been more than about an inch or an inch and a quarter.

All through the world of classical antiquity, all through the Dark and Middle Ages, and all through the Renaissance we had worn shoes which were almost flat. There were just a few exceptions. At the height of Minoan civilization in Crete (about 1400 B.C.), the women had worn high-heeled shoes. They had also worn full flounced skirts, the first example we know of what we could call 'the tea-cosy look' for women's clothes, as opposed to the classical straight-down draped garment comparable with a night-gown.

But this was only for a short period, and only for the women. Certainly in classical tragedy the actor had worn buskins (high thick-soled boots), but this was not a 'heeled' shoe as such; the whole foot was raised, sometimes quite a long way off the floor, but it was still at the same angle as if it were in a flattish sandal. A similar style was seen in the mid 1970s in many of the raised 'platform sole' boots and shoes.

Mediaeval and Renaissance shoes were not as a rule completely flat, they did have the back third of the sole a little raised. But no more than the back of a man's soft bedroom slipper – a little padded thickening. To start putting on a raised, hard heel was quite a different matter, for it altered, however slightly, the balance of the body.

(Courtesans, particularly Venetian courtesans, had worn heels to their shoes long before ordinary men and women, and the fashion-conscious, of course, wore a kind of clog or over-shoe when walking in wet weather to protect their fine shoes from the mud.)

So here we are with heels to our shoes or boots and our centre of gravity slightly more forward even than it had been before. Later on, with the nobility, the heels on their shoes were to be scarlet.

The next great change was not *caused* by these heels, but it would not have happened without them: they were the occasion, if not the cause of it. It was a most amazing change in basic deportment. The upper and upper-middle classes began to walk with their toes turned out. It is now more than fifty years since this walk went out of fashion, and many young people have never seen anyone who walks like that. But for three hundred years (through most of the 17th century, all the 18th and the 19th, and into the beginning of the present century) it was the fashionable walk in Western Europe. Only with the exigencies of the Great War (1914–18) did we return to a natural walk with our feet parallel to each other.

Now, it is obvious that to walk forward with our feet not parallel, is a very uneconomical and silly thing to do. Why ever did we do it? Did we suddenly change from striding about athletically to waddling like ducks? No, it came about indirectly. It happened probably about 1620, at the French Court, which was to be the centre of European fashion for over the next century and a half. There developed a fashionable walk, in which, instead of swinging the legs straight forward as one progressed, one swung each leg outward to the side before bringing it round to the front. Try it yourself and you will discover something: unless you turn the leg and foot *outwards* as you make the swing, you will find the foot turning inwards as you place it down in front, and you will look ridiculous.

The costume historians call this walk 'walking wide', and attribute it to the cavalier boots that were coming into fashion. They were certainly enormous; 'bucket-topped boots' they were called, and often their wide and flaring tops were filled with what looked like a girl's frilly lace petticoat, all frothing up and round the man's leg. But I think this attribution of the boots causing the walk is a mistake. It's putting the cart before the horse. I don't think we choose to wear something and then find we have to move in a certain way. I think we get a new feeling or a new picture of ourselves and then both our clothes and our steps change together.

Whatever the truth of this we certainly *were* taking a new look at ourselves. The focus of the Mediterranean, the centre of civilization for many millennia, had changed to the Atlantic seaboard, and our eyes from now on were westward to the New World.

In the first quarter of the 17th century nearly all our Renaissance dances began to die out. Pavane disappeared, and Galliard died of its later exaggeration. Almain in England lingered on and was danced to some very dull music in the later masques, but finally gave up the ghost with the other two. What survived

was Coranto, but in an unrecognizable form.

We last saw Coranto as it was described by Arbeau (1588) and danced to various Corantos from the Fitzwilliam manuscript (1595). It was then a Farandole line, with the dancers all skipping and hopping in a very light-hearted and carefree way. We meet it again described by de Lauze in 1623, only twenty-eight years later. It could hardly be more different. First of all it is a Danse à Deux as opposed to the old Carole chain; secondly it is an enormously grand dance instead of an informal one; thirdly the music, in triple time, must be taken infinitely slower than the jolly little 6/8 tunes like Pakington's Pownde and Wolsey's Wilde; fourthly the steps are smooth and composed; lastly we get with it the famous instruction 'avec quelque negligence'.

This is to prove a key instruction for the performance of all court dances. From now on we are never to look as if we were making an effort. The energetic athleticism of Galliard was not to make a reappearance.

For the sake of convenience we always refer to the earlier quick springing version of this dance as Coranto, and the smooth, grand Danse à Deux as Courante, or, to make the distinction doubly sure Slow Courante. An interesting point is that in the Baroque Instrumental Suites of J. S. Bach, for instance, both versions appear in different Suites: the obviously quick, old springing version, and the new smoother, slower one. The Slow Courante is in fact the transitional dance which took France from the old, basically Italian technique of the Renaissance to the full flowering of her own French-based Baroque technique.

Slow Courante has two more claims to distinction. It was the dance in which the young Louis XIV, the Sun King, excelled. It was also the dance which established the turned out position of the toes and legs as the norm in orthodox technique. Without this dance and its characteristic movements we might have gone back to parallel feet two hundred and fifty years before we did; in the 1660s instead of the 1910s.

For when in fashionable deportment the outward swing of the leg disappeared, or was modified to the point of hardly being noticeable, the turned out foot and leg remained. (This is the direct cause of the extreme external rotation of both legs in their hip joints which is now one of the characteristics of ballet technique.) This 'turn out', as it is called, is the source of so much misunderstanding that I think it is worth going into its history in some detail. But this necessitates bring-

Le Bal by Abraham Bosse (c. 1635).
The Danse à Deux, showing a transitional stage between Renaissance and Baroque. The new features are better exemplified in the surrounding figures than in the dancing couple. Note their soft lace collars, the heeled-shoe with the over shoe in the right foreground and the bucket-topped boot on the man on the right. The male dancer, however, is shown with his feet parallel and not turned out; this would have been unlikely at this time and in this costume.

Charles II at a Ball at the Hague (1660) by Janssens.
The Danse à Deux in a more developed stage than in Le Bal (Above). Almost certainly Slow Courante. Note the fully turned out legs, though the back foot is too high on the toe, due probably to the artist's licence. Note also Charles' right shoulder in relation to his right foot. They are both forward, in the reverse of 'opposition'. This non-opposition was the body movement which went with the curved walk.

ing to our story a class of people whose existence we have so far neglected to mention. They complicate the straightforward recounting of the development of Western dancing, for their role in it has been so misrepresented and misunderstood that it is quite hard to set the record straight. They are the professionals: not the dancing-masters, the teachers, but the performers.

We have interpreted the word 'popular', not in the old strict sense of the 'people' as opposed to the 'patricians', but in a sense that seems to be more rewarding and fruitful when we are dealing with dancing. 'Popular' we have taken to mean the trend-setting level in any particular age, where the action was, where the new developments took place. This takes us admittedly to court level and aristocratic style between the 12th and the 18th century. But in the 19th century we find ourselves dealing with dance at the level of the bourgeoisie, and today we are happily back with a universal dance-form as we were in the old days of Carole.

What we cannot, with any claim to honesty, include under this title is the work of the professionals. And yet, if we are to give a clear picture, we cannot omit it entirely, for it has caused great complications particularly just at the time we are now describing i.e. the 17th century. It will cause even more in the coming age, the 18th century.

In the Middle Ages and for most of the Renaissance we can dismiss the professionals from serious consideration: from the point of view of dance historians, that is, not from our point of view as human beings. He would be a hard-hearted man who would not feel sympathy, indeed pity, for these poor creatures. They were a pathetic body of people: travelling acrobats, jugglers, and tumblers – general buffoons. The domestic fools, kept in many noble households, must be listed among them, and in most cases they had the best of the bargain, though their role in the establishment was more like that of a pet dog, or a pet monkey, than that of a human being.

This brings us to something which today we find it almost impossible to believe and quite impossible to imagine. They were truly social outcasts, for they were *de facto* (in reality), not always *de jure* (by law), excommunicated from the Church. In a secular age like ours this may not mean very much, but in the Age of Belief, before the Reformation, to be deprived of the Church's Sacraments meant an eternity in hell.

This helps to explain, though not to excuse, the attitude to them of the ordinary population. Their work was not thought of as dancing at all but as tumbling, as 'activity' (the term of early actors for the acrobatic tricks most of them found necessary to hold their audience) and general fooling and buffoonery.

Then in the last decades of the 16th century we begin to see a difference. Acting was beginning to be taken seriously, or rather play-going was. Within Shakespeare's lifetime, troops of performers who at the start had numbered three men and a boy (think of the 'play within the play' in Hamlet), grew to have seventeen members. Among these swelling troops some of our old buffoons found themselves playing the fool to very good purpose.

The next stage in the early 17th century was when groups of them were employed to perform in a concerted action, such as the anti-masque* of the

English Court Masque, and the 'grotesque' work in French Court Ballet. In Italy, these groups formed regular travelling troupes, developing an art form of their own compounded of acrobatic tricks and slapstick comedy – the Commedia dell'Arte. Their careers in England were cut short by the Civil War (1642–51): the absence of a court and therefore of court entertainment, and the closure of the public theatres during the Commonwealth. But in France they flourished, and, under Molière, made tremendous advances as character dancers and comedians.

This is the juncture at which these former tumblers began to affect the development of our dancing. In 1671 Louis XIV permitted them to take on the noble roles in ballet, particularly those roles he had previously danced himself, and to perform such ballets in public, in a theatre. This meant that they would be doing not comical 'grotesque' dances, but the 'noble' technique that the King himself used. In fact, they would share a common technique with the nobility and gentry.

We shall be dealing in the next chapter with French Court Ballet, not for the sake of itself, but for its effect on our general dancing. But at the moment we have come to a critical juncture in the development of dance, and to explain why it is critical we must return to this question of whether we dance with our feet parallel or 'turned out'.

Most histories of ballet claim that the 'turn out' has always been there, though not in form as extreme as we see it today. This is quite untrue. In fact it is essential for all Italian technique, right into the early 17th century, that the basic position of the feet is parallel.

What did happen was that on any occasion when it would be simpler to make a step with a turned out foot and leg the Italians did so. Pieds Croisés (crossed feet), for instance, are steps in which one foot is crossed at right angles in front of the other ankle: it was always made with a turned out foot. What was never done before about the 1620s, was to try to progress forward with one's feet pointing outwards. The main step in later Italian technique, called a Spezzato (described by the dancing-masters Caroso and Negri, c. 1600) still necessitated feet that were as dead parallel as they are in a slow Foxtrot today.

But all these years our tumblers had been turning their legs out, or turning their legs in, or doing anything at all that would help them to look grotesque or give them a safer base for their acrobatic tricks and general high jinks.

So, in the 1660s we get a situation in France in which the professionals were accustomed to a turn out (albeit a grotesque or comic one). The Court had a main noble dance in which the King shone as a performer and this dance incorporated a curved walk that necessitated a turn out. The old Branle, the French form of Carole and still done at court, travelled from side to side not backwards and forwards, and for sideways movements a turn out is a help. Finally our professionals are about to be allowed to dance the noble dances on the stage. For stage use it is a great convenience to be able to move sideways with ease, while yet keeping one's front to the audience.

The scales were hopelessly weighted against the old Italian ideas of fluidity and ordinary good sense. For the next two hundred and fifty years we all walk and dance with our toes turned out.

The splendid century

French Baroque technique late Seventeenth and Eighteenth Century 1661–1789

We come at last to an illustrious era, lasting for just over a century, in which all our earlier developments in dance form reached their ultimate flowering.

It has an orthodox technique, which we call Baroque because of the music which goes with it. This technique developed during the last decades of the 17th century, was in full flower for the first third of the 18th, and in decline from then on until it perished with the French Revolution. The men associated with it were Beauchamps and Pécourt, Louis XIV's great dancing-masters, and Feuillet and Rameau, who published the notation, called stenochoregraphy. The technique

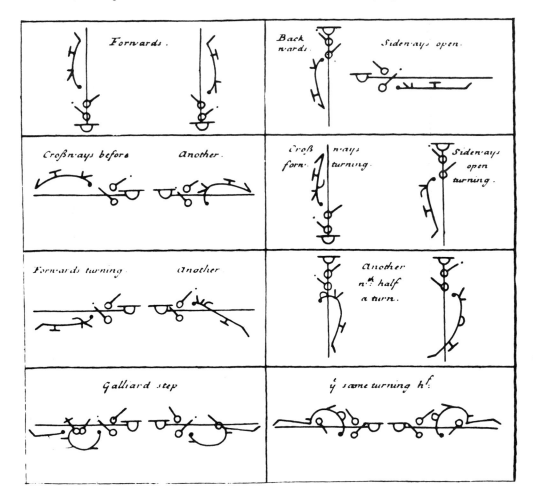

Feuillet's stenochoregraphy. Temps de Courante and the Baroque Pas de Gaillard; this is a quite different step from those in real Renaissance Galliard. Without a verbal key, most people would be at a loss when faced with these symbols.

is sometimes called the Beauchamps-Pécourt or the Feuillet-Rameau technique.

The dances had names some of which are familiar: Minuet, Gavotte, Bourrée Sarabande and Gigue, the numbers of the Baroque Instrumental Suite. Then there were the lesser known ones: Passepieds, Rigaudon, Chaconne, Hornpipe and a good many more. They all share the same technique. Many of the names in the terminology are still in use in Classical Ballet today, but the movements that they then referred to are quite different in most cases from the ones performed today. Even when, as in some of the springing steps, the gross mechanics are the same, the basic placing of the body and style of execution is so dissimilar that the result seems a different thing.

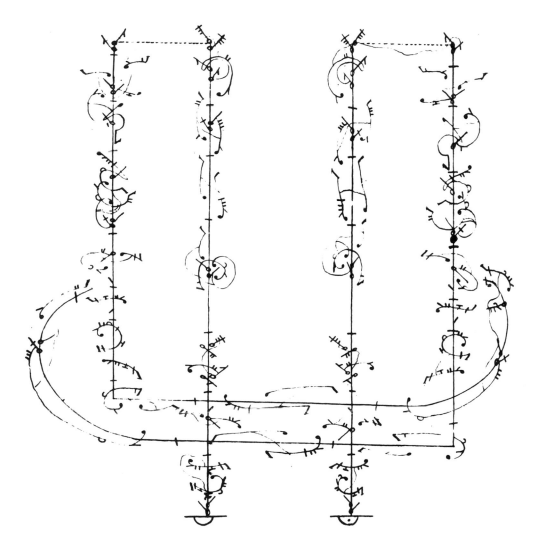

Feuillet notation used to denote both the steps and the track of a duet for two men. The floor track is easily discerned but the step signs need a good deal of construing.

This technique and style of dancing, 'the French style', was shared by the court, the upper and middle classes (in fact by everyone above the folk level) and by the newly enfranchised professionals. We have told, in the previous chapter, how from 1671 the professionals were allowed to perform the 'noble numbers' instead of being limited to their old character roles. The most distinguished of them now played the part of the 'danseur noble' in their ballets. The title is still applied to the leading men in a ballet company.

So here we have a situation in which we get an authoritative technique controlled from Paris, shared by both amateurs and professionals, and lasting for over a hundred years. What was it like?

It was danced in shoes with a low heel but a very thin flexible sole – little soft pumps. The legs were turned out in the hip-joints, but not more than could be held easily and honestly, without any kind of unnatural twisting – nothing like the amount of 'turn out' in ballet today. For the first time we have set arm movements to all the steps; not just set, but very strictly ruled indeed.

✳ Baroque retains the old rise and fall of Domenico's technique, but elaborates it. 'The Movement', as it is still called, has now a preliminary sink, a bend of both knees but with the weight on only one foot, followed by a rise and a return to the normal level. So whereas a Movimento in Domenico was 'rise and sink to the level', Baroque is 'sink down below the level, rise above it and sink to the level'.

The position of having both knees bent with the feet level but the weight on only one foot is called a 'plié sous soi', a 'fold of the leg' underneath oneself. The position on the rise is more unusual. The foot of the supporting leg is on the low quarter point and the knee of course is braced; the other leg, equally braced, is held firmly against it, rather like a splint, with its foot pulled up almost at right

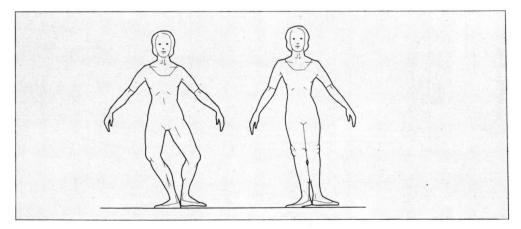

Left: Plié sous soi.   Right: The equilibrium.

The King's Grand Ball by Rameau.
The Danse à Deux at the height of its development. Note the dispositions in the room: the King in front, slightly raised, the Princesses and court ladies sitting on each side in an oval, with the courtiers behind them, and the musicians at the far end from the Presence. The four figures on the floor have confused many. They represent only one couple, shown first (halfway down the room) bowing to the King, and then at the far end ready to start the dance.

angles. This has been called 'a flat iron foot' by so distinguished a person as Madame Kasarvina. The phrase exactly describes it.

This unusual position is called 'the equilibrium'. This is a technical term, meaning of course the balance. The position is fundamental to the technique, for if one neglects to achieve it on every single rise one makes, one's dancing lacks the

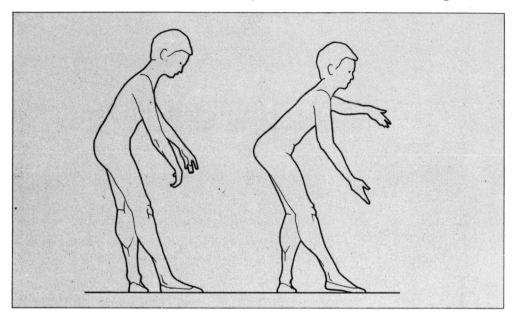

The Bow that went with Baroque technique. Right and wrong version.

necessary bite and edge, and seems merely flabby. At the same time it must only be a momentary passing through of the position. To hold it for any appreciable time would look stiff and awkward.

The Baroque equivalent of the old Simple is a step moving from a plié sous soi to the equilibrium, and sinking to the level again preparatory to repeating the step. This step, a combination of plié sous soi, equilibrium and sink, is called a 'demi-coupé'. It is the key step to the whole technique, for it is the opening movement of nearly all the non-jumped combined steps. It is as important as the long, slow, gliding step with a rise at the end in Foxtrot today. Once you have mastered either, you can dance that technique. It is literally a case of 'ce n'est que le premièr pas qui coutê'. (It is only the first step that counts.)

The equivalent of a Domenico Double is a step called a Fleuret. Here we have an opening demi-coupé but without a sink at the end; keep up on the equilibrium and take two small 'pas marchés' (walking steps) on the balls of the feet before you sink again to the level. The Fleuret is the most popular step of Baroque technique just as Doubles were in the Renaissance.

The quality of 'Aierc' (resilience) is as important in Baroque as in Renaissance technique, but during this period we begin to call it 'Balon'. What had to be sacrificed, as we explained in the last chapter, was Maniera. The old flowing contra-body movement was made impossible by the turn out of the legs.

They tried to make up for this by emphasizing the opposition of the arm movements. If one were standing with the left foot in front, the right arm would be raised, forward and upward, through 90° from the elbow, and the left arm would make a little sympathetic movement from the wrist in imitation. (Illust. 1)

If one were making steps like demi-coupés or fleurets in which there was a

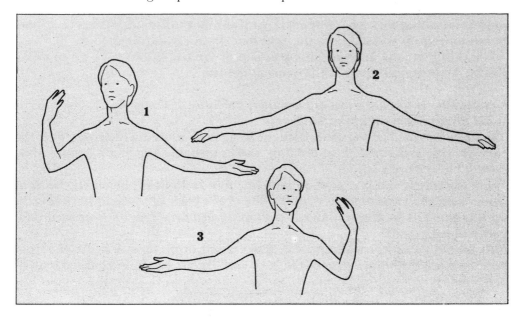

Basic arm movement of Baroque technique. Simple change to opposition.

change of foot, one's arms came down to a neutral position (Illust. 2) and then the opposite arm came up from the elbow. (Illust. 3) In a step that did not give a change of foot, the high forearm and the low hand did not retrace their tracks back to neutral, but continued on and made a complete circle, the high arm circling from the elbow, the low one from the wrist. These are just two of the basic arm movements, simple change to opposition, and circling to opposition. There are more complicated ones, but they all stress the opposition of the arms to the forward leg. They also mark the beat of the music, and help one to balance. Once the arm movements are mastered it is much easier to dance *with* them than without them.

The one dance where we do not get these opposition arms is Minuet. Minuet has, like Waltz in Ballroom today, a special step of its own which, although it is done in classically orthodox technique, is unique to this particular rhythm. It consists of a demi-coupé and a fleuret done to six counts, or two beats of 3/4 Minuet music. The time is ♩ ♪ | ♩ ♩ ‖, the weight changes coming down on 1,3,4, and 5, giving the rhythm slow, quick, quick, slow. (It is also a splendid example of hemiola; this is the practice in music of playing two bars of 3/4 time as if it were three bars of 2/4. Hemiola is always fascinating, for the balance of 2 against 3 has a particular attraction for our human sense of rhythm.)

All the steps in Minuet begin with the right foot, both for the man and the girl. It is the last dance we have that still shows its Branle origins in this way, and after Minuet all our dances have partners using the opposite feet, or 'mirror' feet, as we do today.

Being based on a Branle, which of course travels to the left, we would expect to start with the left foot, as any Branle normally would. But in its later stages, the Branle de Poitou, from which Minuet developed, began its step from the second position (standing with one's feet apart, with one foot to the side of the other) and its first movement was made by the right foot closing in to join the left.

It was at this time that the basic positions of the feet began to be given numbers by Beauchamps, Louis' chief dancing-master.

First position: is when the feet are together, touching at the heels.
Second position: the feet apart, but level.
Third position: the feet together, with the front heel crossed a little way over the back. This is a classical third position, and is crossed over much less than the present ballet third position.
Fourth position: is an open position with one foot in front of the other, the front foot crossed the same amount over the line of the back as it would have been in third position. This classical fourth position is also very much less crossed than fourth in ballet today.
Fifth position: The feet together, this time crossed more than in third, the front heel touching the big toe joint of the back foot. Again, much less crossed than in ballet today.

The interesting thing about the numbering of the feet positions is how it displays the French attitude of mind – the second position is with the foot to the side as in the Branle. Had the numbering taken place in Italy, almost certainly, second position would have been with the foot in front as in Farandole, and fourth would have been with the feet side by side. ⌘

The Minuet is a unique dance for other reasons than that it had a step of its own. It also has a set form which lasted, with only minor modifications and revisions, for over a century. There is an interesting story in connection with this.

When Louis XIV, in 1661 allowed a clique of his dancing-masters to persuade him to found a Royal Academy of Dancing, they hoped to get a strangle-hold on the art and prevent all their rivals from teaching at all, or certainly from having any influence at court. Their French authoritarian minds planned a future in which each of the main dance rhythms had one set form, arranged and authorized by them, and that only they should be allowed to teach these.

They succeeded in their aim with only one dance, Minuet. So we have actually *the* Minuet, but not *the* Gavotte, *the* Bourrée, or *the* Sarabande, all of which had multifarious versions. Minuet, too, has many so-called 'figured' versions, designed for stage or court ballet. But the straight ballroom version has only one form which lasted throughout the whole of the 18th century, in most of Western Europe, but particularly France and England.

It is, of course, a Danse à Deux, and it has four main figures.

1 The opening figure: leading the lady into the dance.
2 The famous Z pattern figure: revised from Pécourt from a previous S figure.

3 The one handed figure: the couple going round each other, first by the right and then by the left hand.

4 The closing figure: where the man leads the girl round with both hands.

It is really more a ritual performance than a dance in the sense that Italian Bassa Danza or Slow Courante were dances.

One word of warning. The real dance bears no resemblance to the Romantic visions of Minuet we see in 'costume' plays, and films, and sometimes on television. What has come down to us as 'traditional' are the 19th-century versions of all these dances. We will go into the reason for this later. In the meantime should you want to understand the difference in the two styles you should play the Duke of Plaza-Toro's Gavotte from Gilbert and Sullivan's The Gondoliers, and then perhaps the Minuet from Bach's Second Orchestral Suite. The dance differences – technique, form and style – are every bit as fundamental as the musical ones.

One popular howler about Minuet is still regularly perpetrated: that the 'menu' of its French name 'menuet', means small, and that the steps therefore must be small and mincing. The derivation is quite wrong. The names comes from the Branle à Mener de Poitou, the 'led Branle', and refers to the man 'leading the lady'. The wrong belief has had lamentable effects on the performance of the dance though, and on our ideas about it and on the whole of Baroque dance style. It has reduced it to the 'powder and patch Rococo-ry' of some women historical novelists. The kind of person who would think Minuet was mincing would think of Mozart as dainty.

Marie Antoinette and her brothers dancing at Schonbrunn by De Vinck. True Baroque dance style. Note the simplicity and lack of affectation.

Left: A mid-19th-century ballet imitation of a ball at Versailles with Fanny Elssler 'en travestie' as the Sun King. But it was a travesty of the dance also. Note the absurd affectation of both figures, and the lack of balance and restraint. This is the style that has come down to us as 'traditional'.

Right: A typical children's 'Minuet' as taught today. Very charming little dancers but it should be made clear that they come from fairy tale land and not from history.

The triumphant heretic

England 1610–1812

When Charles II returned to England at his restoration in 1760 he brought with him the 'French dances', which he had learnt during his exile abroad. Pepys saw him dancing these early in the 1660s and was most impressed. 'Very noble it was,' he said, 'and great pleasure to see.'

A year or two later Pepys went to Whitehall again to watch the Court dancing, but this time found the French dances very tedious. This is typical of the ambivalent English attitude to a great deal of French culture at its most characteristic. We find their classic playwright Racine a high old bore, and even think Molière would be improved with a bit more humanity. The French for their part consider Shakespeare barbarous and the English liking for mixed art forms like tragi-comedy typical of our uncultivated tastes, incapable as we are of appreciating the pure crystalline essence of their art.

'The further off from England, the nearer is to France – then turn not pale, beloved snail, but come and join the dance.' This expresses very well the 'entente' between England and France in the 17th and 18th centuries. It was certainly not 'cordiale'. But in the end join in the dance we all did, though just who joined in which dance gives us food for thought.

The Court balls at Whitehall, which Pepys attended, opened with a set of French Branles, before the French dances proper that we have already mentioned. But they finished the evening by doing English Country Dances. Charles always enjoyed these. 'Ah, the dance of old England', he said, about Cuckolds all a Row!

French Baroque technique, however, was thought of as the height of social attainment in the field of dancing. All the dancing-masters taught it and continued to do so throughout the 18th century. Compared with such cultivated elegance the English Country Dance seemed a poor relation. When, in 1700, Feuillet published his notation of the French technique to be followed in 1706 by Weaver's translation, it seemed to have reached a plateau of perfection that was thought of as being permanent and for the rest of time.

Alas for human conceit in these matters! The complacency and condescension of its practitioners and admirers were ill-founded. But to see what happened to it we must cross the Channel again and take up our residence in Versailles where life was 'un ballet continuel' of which the choreography was etiquette.

I have tried my best to escape from the question of court ballet in this short account of our dancing past. It is a subject which has engendered so much colourful romance in our ballet books that an enormous demolition job will be needed before we can ever see it clearly. But I cannot avoid mentioning it at last so it will be best if we get a few things quite clear.

Court ballet was not some strange, exotic growth, dreamed up by the public relations department of Renaissance princes and subsequent monarchs. It was a ceremonial activity much more comparable with the Trooping of the Colour than such theatrical works as Swan Lake or Les Sylphides.

Of course it involved beautiful dancing, as the Trooping involves beautiful marching, but then our forefathers *did* dance beautifully. Not only did they dance beautifully, but their dances were suitable to be put straight into such a ceremony, as ours today are not. From Domenico on, probably from 12th-century Provence on, the main dances at court had been Danses à Deux, or à Trois, or à Quatre, and so on; i.e. dances that occupy the whole dance floor and were an equal pleasure to those dancing and to those watching.

Such dances had only to be put into an allegorical or mythological framework, dressed in lovely clothes symbolically decorated, and we had the main structure of a court ballet. The songs, the poems, the declamation, all added to this effect. What in the earlier days had been the unstructured buffoonery of the domestic fools before the performance, became formalized into the English anti-masque, and elaborated into the comic entrées of French ballet. By the time Louis XIV was thirty-three, in 1671, it had all become very elaborate, particularly the scenery.

What we find it difficult to understand today is that what made it genuine, the essence of it, was the presence of the monarch, the Prince or the Lord. It was a ceremony, not just a show: something actual, something real. The dancers too, at least the noble ones, not the comic professionals, were taking part in a ritual, however implicit the ritual quality had now become.

Because in the West the early Christian Fathers had always turned their faces against any kind of dance in our Church Liturgy, we have no explicitly sacramental dance forms in Western Europe. The nearest we have ever come to dance as a direct means of grace was in early court ballet. Admittedly the ambiance there was classical and pagan, but Mediaeval and Renaissance allegory is compounded of an amalgam of pagan and Christian beliefs.

It was therefore treachery of a subtle kind when Louis succumbed to the persuasions of his dancing-masters and his musicians (chiefly Lully) and allowed them to stage an imitation of this ceremony with professionals standing in for him and his courtiers. He preferred to be impersonated by a professional who was of no importance at all, a complete outsider, rather than that his place should be taken, in the normal run of things, by one of the younger princes of the blood. Can you imagine the Queen deciding the Trooping is really too much bother, and getting a set of film extras (they'd naturally have to know how to manage a horse) to ride in for the Royal Family, and another larger set to stand in for the guards?

The irony of it is that it was all to no avail. For little more than a generation, until 1708, the professionals were content to provide a copy of the real thing, sharing their technique with the courtiers. Then they began to whittle away the whole basis of noble dancing. Two quite different sets of them attacked it on two different flanks. On the left came the advance guard of the Romantic Revolution which was to engulf all the arts at the end of the century. These, on the whole, were sensitive and well-meaning people. They wanted dancing to be expressive of real human emotion. We have been hearing this plea for expressiveness on and off ever since; in the present century by Isadora Duncan, the central European School of Jooss and Laban, and all the schools of American modern dance.

The trouble with all these romantics is their limitation of outlook. The central Europeans and Martha Graham, wanted to express *Angst* in a raw form, hitherto not seen in dancing. The 18th-century female version of Isadora, Marie Sallé, almost certainly wanted to express an emotional yearning for some kind of dreamland. All these protesters seem incapable of understanding that the orthodox technique of the dancing of any age *does* express something, though it may not be something that they can comprehend or sympathize with.

Baroque technique expressed the calm Olympian quality of French classical thought. It is the dance equivalent of the dramatic style of Corneille and Racine. (As such, it is easy to see why the English disliked it. They were never very good at it.) But the attempts to make it emotionally expressive, in the Romanticist sense, not only tore the style to shreds but removed it irrevocably to a theatrical setting and divorced it for good from that vital half of it that had flourished in ordinary social life.

The attack on the right flank can be explained much more easily and quickly. It was made by dancers of the opposite type from our Romanticists. They simply wanted to show off. We must remember that they were descended from players whose livelihood had depended on their ability to attract attention to themselves. They found it hard to identify with the aristocratic attitudes of 'avec quelque negligence': a creed that holds if you can't do a thing with apparent effortlessness then you mustn't do it at all.

The damage they did was enormous. Insidiously, step by step, they inserted into the noble technique more and more of their old tumblers' tricks. The beats, the turns, the general capering and carry on. It led to two very sad results. The first was a musical one. Baroque technique was supremely rhythmical. The arcs of the floor track traced by the dancers corresponded with the main phrases of the music, and the rise and fall of their bodies matched the dynamic nuances of the shorter phrases. Next time you listen to the dance rhythms of Bach or Handel imagine how this could be a kind of visual extra line to the musical arrangement.

But beats, turns and capers, like acrobatic tricks, dictate their own dynamics. At least the harder ones do. Their rhythms are not the subtle nuances of the Baroque Dance Suite (in fact many of these tours de force never found their rhythmic match until we get to Tchaikovsky at the end of the last century). In the opinion of many, the misguided virtuosity of the 18th-century professionals first caused the belief that all dancers are inherently unmusical. (Unfortunately, with far too many, it is true.)

The second effect is harder to explain today as we no longer think in the categories of class. But it still is true that if something connected with an admired set of people is adopted by an unadmired set, the first group tend to drop and finally to dissociate themselves from it.

This is what happened, not just to the Baroque technique itself, but actually to the Danse à Deux.

The nobility saw the dances, in which they had excelled for so long, being vulgarized on stage by these inharmonious exaggerations. They themselves began to dance them less and less, and though the Danse à Deux did survive until the Revolution, chiefly in the form of Minuet, the old convention of all the

A ball at St. James's on the King's birthday.
Late 18th-century Minuet; by this time, one of a series which would open the ball. By earlier standards very bad style because of the raised arms.

main dances being in this form died out. Finally, the opening Branles disappeared too, and we are left with a set of Minuets to open the ball, and then dances of a very different kind. Yes, you have probably guessed. The country cousin, that poor relation, the English Country Dance! The one form that in the 17th century had stood out against the tyranny of the 'French dances' now triumphed at their demise.

The French translated the form into their own version, the Contre Danse, and later we get a German version, the Contre Danse à l'Allemagne. Across the Atlantic there were also the Contra dances in New England (still to be found alive and well). The French exported several dances back to England, but in particular the Cotillion, a square dance for four couples, standing each couple on one side of the square facing inwards. The music was lively and not like the early English square dances which must have influenced them – particularly the four couple dances of the 17th century Hunsdon House, Never Love thee more, Lull me beyond thee which had, as their titles suggest, slow and beautiful ballads as their airs. Many of the musical world of today would find the earlier English music of a far finer quality than the French quadrilles which were to

Le Bal Paré.
The Contre Danse Allemande, a typical large square for eight, showing the high arm movements that came back in the late 18th century.

Right: A 19th-century re-drawing of the central figure in Le Bal Paré, often reproduced in dance histories as Minuet. There are so many errors they would be hard to enumerate. The most dangerous is the translation of the original poise into a flaccid lack of conviction.

follow. The Cotillion was to last in England for a very long time, well into living memory, especially in country places. For a brief period in the late 19th century, as the 'Cotillon', it degenerated to a rather silly party game for London society with forfeits and prizes.

Once again America also was to adopt the Cotillion, either through its settlers or its transatlantic travellers. They kept the old name of 'square dance', though Cotillion was used for a while. The Quadrille and the Lancers (a quadrille with its own name and figures) lasted in the United Kingdom for well over a century. In places, particularly Ireland and Scotland, they are danced still. But the effect of the Quadrille paled into insignificance compared with the shattering impact that was to be made on our Western ways by the next change in our dance habits. We must brace ourselves for that. We shall need to.

The 18th-Century English Assembly Rooms

'Full fifteen centuries before
Beau Nash controlled the Pump-room floor,
* With world and wife to follow,*
The Romans, bathers through and through,
The worth of Bath's ablutions knew
* And there rejoiced to wallow.'*

from Punch. 'County Songs' by E. V. Lucas

Where Roman colonial society from the 2nd to the 4th centuries met to indulge in bathing and conversation, our native forefathers in the 18th assembled not to bathe but to dance.

Assembly Rooms are a feature of English life in the 18th century which had a strong influence on our style of dancing. French dancing was focused on the Court, and the smaller courts of Western Europe, particularly the German duchies and principalities, all kept an emulous eye on Versailles, ready to ape the latest fashion. Not so the English, as so often sturdily independent.

Once we got rid of the male Stuart dynasty with the 'Glorious Revolution' of 1688, the Whig aristocracy began to take over the direction of English taste and manners. By the time Queen Anne was dead they were well in control, and four successive German kings, all called George, did nothing to challenge their supremacy. As far as fashion was concerned no English monarch, with the exception of Edward VII and Edward VIII, was ever again to be in the lead.

Our admired model from now on was the English gentleman living on his country estate; this was later to be landscaped by one of our great English gardeners, and to have a Palladian mansion decorated by the Adam brothers and furnished by one of that trio of geniuses, Chippendale, Sheraton and Hepplewhite. In visual taste it was a high spot of all time; their classical sanity had spared us the vulgarities of Continental Rococo.

The Assembly Rooms at York, designed by that great art patron Lord Burlington himself, are a perfect example of Palladio's principles of proportion; but here they were too pedantically applied, for the space between the pillars is too narrow for a hooped skirt. More important the dancing floor is narrow in proportion to its length. This influenced the design for many of our Assembly Rooms.

This is probably the reason for the prevalence of the 'longways' Country Dance in 18th-century England, as opposed to the 'large square' which the French adapted for their Contre Danses Anglaises and Allemandes, and Cotillons. Indeed it was in these French versions that the 'large square' came back into fashion in England and subsequently became the Quadrille.

The shape of the dancing space dictated which of the forms of the 'New Country Dance' tended to be fashionable at any period. The 'small square' for four, e.g. Heart's Ease, perfectly fitted the rooms of the Stuart houses in the 17th century. It was this kind of dance, done at home, that the serving-maid would be bidden to join to make up the number. But for a large gathering, like a subscription ball at the Assembly Rooms, the longways set 'for as many as will' suited both the numbers present and the space available.

These are the dances we read about in Jane Austen. By her time the introductory Minuets – a series of Danses à Deux over which at Bath Beau Nash had exercised great tyranny – had disappeared. Here are the English gentry disporting themselves, tracing patterns up and down the set which harmonized perfectly with the curves of their Adam ceilings and their Chippendale chairs.

(What a pity that for two generations of Englishwomen of this century this style is thought of only as a gymnastic substitute for school hockey or lacrosse on afternoons too wet for outdoor games!)

The Century of Waltz

1812–1912

'Le Congrès ne marche pas – il danse', said the Prince de Ligne, of the Congress of Vienna. ('Congress isn't working – it's dancing.') In 1815 the whole of Western Europe was dancing too, and the dance was the Waltz.

The advent of Waltz in Polite Society was quite simply the greatest change in dance form and dancing manners that has happened in our history. It was preceded by, or coincided with, fundamental changes in Western civilization. Some historians have now begun to think of this period as the second great change in the history of mankind, the first being that between the old and the new stone-age; that was when we first settled down and tried to produce food instead of wandering over the face of the earth hunting it.

The shot by the 'embattled farmers' at Concorde in 1775, that started the American War of Independence, coincided with a triple revolution, political, imaginative, and material. The greatest, single political event was the French Revolution. This marked the end of the Ancien Régime, the end of the old noblesse, and the end of French court dancing. From now on dancing became a bourgeois activity, and aristocratic style was seen only in stage imitations, some of it ludricrously off target.

The romantic revolt in the arts caused what Sir Isaiah Berlin has called 'a shift of consciousness'. From now on we accept that the cultivation of an individual sensibility is the prime aim of the artist, and that the object of the arts is not the ordering of our emotions but their excitation.

Finally, there was the Industrial Revolution. Whereas its obvious material achievements have been recognized, its effects on our minds and nerves have not yet been considered seriously.

Waltz reflected and exemplified many of these changes. That in Polite Society a man should actually put his arm round a girl when he danced with her was nothing short of scandalous to the older generation. Peasant dancing has always involved arms round waists and general jollity, but where was that sort of thing going to stop? And the couple were not even side by side, but opposite each other! (They were usually not very close, in actual fact.) Not only indecent, but vulgar! So much for the social aspect of the new dances.

But the psychological aspect of the 'closed' position of the dancing couple was even more important than its reputed indecency. For centuries Polite Society had danced in a way which had kept the extrovert-introvert tendencies in human nature in beautiful balance. The Danse à Deux was a perfect example of 'inclu-

LORD WORCESTER.   LADY JERSEY.   CLANRONALD MACDONALD.   LADY WORCESTER.

Above: *First Quadrille danced at Almack's*. Note the change in deportment: the feet high on the toes, the Romantic curve of Lady Jersey's body, and the Byronic appearance of Clanronald Macdonald.

Below: Drawing from Thomas Wilson's Treatise of Waltzing. A very genteel version of early waltz. Note the foot going up very high on the toe.

sive mutuality', the pleasure of the dancing couple being reinforced by the pleasure of their watching friends, and vice versa.

Now we get the two dancers, not only in each other's arms, but turned inwards, towards each other, and cut off from, though surrounded by, a throng of similarly closed couples.

The fact that they are all rotating endlessly and rapidly adds one more irrational feature to the scene: not quite Eastern dervishes in a state of trance, but well on the way to it. Most important of all was the rhythm. Waltz rhythm is the rhythm of a swing – strong, weak, weak, or more accurately, very strong, weak, medium: what Rudolf von Laban called 'impulse, swing, tension'.

Hold your arm out to your side at shoulder level, and let it swing across in front of you and back again while you sing any waltz tune, taking one bar to each arc of the swing. You will see that the first beat comes as gravity takes over, pulling the arm down; it is a very strong beat. The second beat comes as the arm swings up effortlessly, though against gravity; it is a very light one. The third beat is the most interesting of all; it comes when the arm is momentarily still. The impulse from the drop is just about to be exhausted, but gravity has not yet taken over for the next drop. For a fascinating moment the arm is poised motionless in the air, without our having to hold it there with any noticeable muscle force.

It is their subtle understanding of this third beat that gives the true Viennese lilt to Waltz playing; though the tempo may be fast, they still don't seem to be rushed. Compared to this, many English bands sound both leaden-footed and in a tearing hurry.

Waltz rhythm has, I think, caused a fundamental modification of our rhythmic sense. It is such a hypnotic rhythm, even when badly played, and it went on as the main dance rhythm in the West for so long, over a century, that it is not perhaps surprising. Its neglect of the second beat in the bar is the difficulty here. Many of the earlier triple rhythms (for example Branle Gai, Tordion, and Galliard) depend absolutely on the second beat being as much stressed as the first, in all the odd numbered bars. A conductor who plays these early dances in waltz rhythm, even bad waltz rhythm, is impossible to dance to. On the other hand, the even numbered bars *need* to be played with a swing. So if one has a conductor who is consciously *resisting* any influence from waltz rhythm, the result tends to be wooden throughout.

Of the later triple rhythms Sarabande does usually get the second beat stress that it requires, but it is very rarely played with enough momentum (as distinct from *speed*), to prevent sagging. Minuet is a problem on its own, but at least it is usually taken seriously as music. Not always though. In a Covent Garden production in the 1960s, the famous Minuet from Handel's Alcino was played like a Waltz, and the Royal Ballet Opera Group waltzed happily and shamelessly to it.

Queen Victoria and Prince Albert as Queen Philippa and Edward III by Landseer.
The Victorian view of the Middle Ages. This beautiful piece of painting sets the tone of the 'Balmoralised' Mediaevalism of the rest of the century.

The Waltz is basically a work rhythm. It was the first work rhythm that we ever accepted above the level of folk dance. Many folk dances have formalized work rhythms, and all our dance rhythms had their root sources in peasant cultures. But from Branle Double on, the rhythms we had so far adopted were all what might be called 'ritual' rhythms, i.e. they did not correspond with any materially useful action. They were in fact pure dance. Until we come to Waltz.

Not that the Ländler, the German peasant dance from which Waltz came, was a specific work dance. Nor is Waltz specific to one single working action. There are dozens of working actions that can be done to it, but particularly anything that requires a good wallop on the first beat, and then a recovery period, e.g. hammering, or digging up the road. Try swinging a pick to Minuet and you won't get much work done, but you can swing a pick splendidly to Waltz.

So in the wake of a political, romantic and industrial revolution, we had a completely new dance form and new dance rhythm that perfectly suited the new conditions of life, socially, psychologically and materially. It both reflected the new standards, and satisfied the new needs. Is it any wonder it was such an overwhelming success?

There is little more to say about Waltz. We went on Waltzing right into the present century and the eve of the first world war. Latterly we begin to get the tempo eased a little from the old sixty plus bars a minute to round about forty plus. The Waltz music from Merry Widow encouraged the easier tempo (though bad bands always tend to play fast to make up for their lack of real rhythm).

The Waltz is still with us today.

The only other dance rhythm worth mentioning is Polka. This came from Bohemia, our present Czechoslovakia, and grew popular from the 1840s on. It was a jolly little dance, with a very energetic jump, done in single couples like Waltz. It was the first of a series of importations from Eastern Europe of various national dances, like Mazurkas from Poland and Czardas from Hungary. But Polka was the only one to have any lasting popularity. Their rhythms were highly infectious, though they may have proved a little too exotic to make them seem at home in Victorian England or the France of the second Empire.

As a solid background to all this giddy turning in Waltz, or hopping about in Polka, we had the last two stages of the communal dance – Quadrille, and later in the century, Lancers.

These were the 19th-century developments of the large square for eight that had constituted the French Contre Danse Anglaise and Contre Danse Allemande. (The 18th-century French Cotillon had now become a sort of party game.) But, compared with the pre-revolutionary dances, the Quadrille and Lancers had no fundamental dance rhythms of their own and simply used the marches and gallops that the Strauss family provided in such abundance for this purpose, imitated by dozens of industrious hacks.

It is sad that our English Country Dance had completely disappeared from fashionable society; the old airs and figures were rescued by Cecil Sharp, founder of the English Folk Dance Society, with the devoted help of Maud Karpeles and other devotees and the work of such musicians as Vaughan Williams.

But what *was* accepted by the fashionable world was Scottish dancing. During

Polka as a national dance.

Polka as a ballroom dance.

Top: Victorian urban society at a ball.   Bottom: Victorian village life – somewhat idealized.

Right: Probably a Galop showing a great sense of movement.

the second half of the century, whether due to the influence of Queen Victoria and Balmoral or not, it became both popular and chic. Strathspeys and Reels resounded through the ballrooms of Debrett, and were used for diversion and home recreation even by such out and out intellectuals as the Strachey family.

The music is enlivening of course, but there are two interesting things to note about Scottish dancing. The footwork strongly resembles the footwork of the springing steps in old French Baroque technique. (Was this the Auld Alliance turning up again?) The exception to this is the use of the bent knee, particularly in Strathspey, which Beauchamps and Pécourt would never have tolerated. But

the spring and verve, and the masculinity of the old style are still there, and when well done, still a joy to behold.

And with 'masculinity' we come to the second point. Scottish dancing in Highland dress is the last dance style in which a Western man can look really splendid, in the sense that our Renaissance, Cavalier, and Augustan forefathers looked really splendid. We hardly ever see such splendid sights today. For in the Romantic Revolution something very sad happened to Western man. He began to lose his choreographic identity.

To find out how this happened we must go back to the professional dancers in France at the end of the 18th century during the time of the Revolution and the Napoleonic wars – the thirty odd years from 1789 to 1820.

We have said that French Baroque technique, the old noble style of dancing, had been destroyed by two contrasting schools of thought among the professional ballet dancers. The romanticists had wanted to make dancing emotionally expressive and capable of telling a story without words. The virtuosi had simply wanted to show off, and make it an occasion for displaying their physical expertise like circus performers – both aims anathema to a lover of the classic style.

One more factor was to combine with the above two before we got a mix from which there emerged ballet technique as we know it today. This third element was provided by the contemporary interest in imitating Greek sculpture, and the movement in art that we call Neo-Classicism.

One of the odder outcomes of these new classical leanings was the fashion among society women of posing, for their guest's entertainment, as statues. The most notorious of these posers was Lord Nelson's mistress, Lady Hamilton. While she was still slender, she must have looked very lovely in the light draperies of the time. In the ballet these light draperies had already replaced much more concealing garments of the pre-revolutionary era. For the first time since Botticelli and Leonardo we were able to see the line of the girl's thigh through her skirts. The sculptural poses were now to become not just one feature of the technique of ballet, but in time the all-important feature. The word 'line' in ballet now means the line of the dancer's body.

But the light draperies and the extension of the arms and legs in the air encouraged something in ballet that divorced it even further from its old roots in noble dancing. This was the notion that they should pretend that they were flying. Human beings can't fly of course, but that didn't stop them trying to pretend that they could. Sometimes they even used wires, as in Peter Pan today. By now I would estimate that about three-quarters of the effort – and gruelling effort it is – that goes to making a ballet dancer is concerned with trying to make the body look weightless and airborne.

In their attempts to achieve this airborne look they went higher and higher up on their toes. Finally of course, the women went right up on to the ends of their toes – the position called 'on point'. But the difference between being on point and being on a high three-quarter point is very slight except for the extra muscular effort involved. The principle of natural leverage in the foot has already been eroded by the time one reaches the three-quarter point stage. The foot is then rigid and incapable of any 'give'. The old 'sprung' quality, the wonderful lift and shock absorption were sacrificed for the appearance of looking light.

In thus sacrificing a mechanical principle for a mere appearance the ballet was doing only what all the other art forms were to indulge in throughout the 19th century. You could not have a greater contrast to the Renaissance mind.

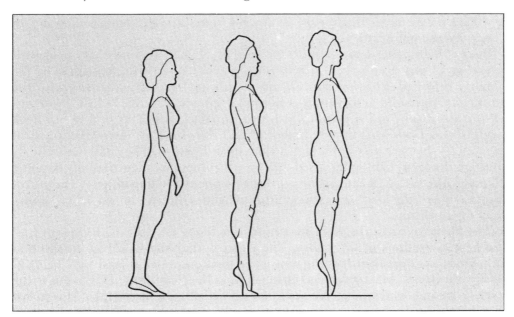

The foot position changing from the old, sprung, quarter point through to a full, rigid point.

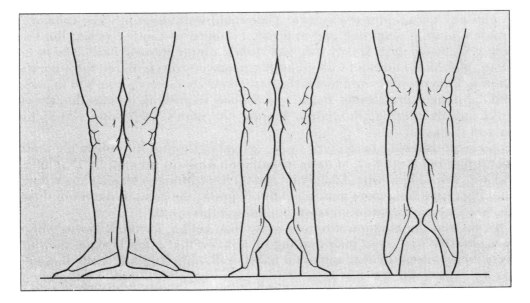

The same progression from a low, sprung foot to a high, rigid point, this time with the legs turned out.

('Show me how it *works*', said Leonardo.) But this 'tippy-toe' attitude to our feet carried over into social dancing, and grown men and women tried to dance all the time 'on their toes'. They thereby reduced their normal foot leverage to such an extent that they had to bend their knees to provide enough 'give' to their movements, and we develop in Western deportment the weak, unbraced knee and slack pelvic girdle that we see all around us today. In the process our centre of gravity had gone right back.

By the 1820s ballet was a purely theatrical art. It had no longer any links with court life, or any need to conceive its roles as ever being performed again by the nobility. Most professional dancers are a little undersized compared with the admired social build at any time. A normal sized person tends to look enormous on the stage. The old supernatural figures in classical ballets had been Greek Gods. Greek Gods are not only immortal, but they have an interesting physical attribute – they are a little bit bigger than mere humans. They can naturally fly through the air at lightening speed, but we never imagine them actually flapping about as they do so. (Renaissance angels never seemed to flap either.) The god in the machine (the *deus ex machina*) always comes down on his cloud either standing or sitting.

The old supernatural setting gave in fact no scope for the new technique and the new aspirations of the ballet. The irony is that the world of Apollo and Dionysus were ditched just at the time when their costumes at least were being at their most Greek. The setting was changed from the clear light of Olympus to the dark Germanic woodlands. We are in for an age of wilis and sylphs. It is to last for a long time. In the literature of the early 19th century two of the great romantic figures are the unattainable female and the fated and tormented male, e.g. 'La belle dame sans merci' and the 'palely loitering' knight at arms. These became the stereotypes of the female and male leading roles in romantic ballet.

This was splendid for the women. They could waft about in white tulle and tarlatan, looking weightless and as if they belonged-to another world. But the men got a rotten deal. If only they had chosen a more Byronic hero! The technique, high on the toes and with very soft arm movements, favoured the women's dancing from the start. Add to this the lamentable characters a man had to play, and the result is predictable. Ballet, and dancing in general, became thought of as effeminate. Finally, in western Europe, the man's parts were played by women in travesti.

All might still have been saved by the arrival in western Europe, in the years just before the great war, of those magnificent Russians brought by Diaghilev. Fokine's Prince Igor, with Adolf Bolm and all those Mongols leaping about him, could not have been more masculine. But Nijinsky, the greatest dancer of them all, was a strange uncanny creature, not quite of this world.

In the end the situation was even worse than before, for the Russians' enormous artistry had given their dancing such kudos that other kinds of dancing were thought meretricious, and as for ballet, well, only Russians could dance it.

King Edward VII and Queen Alexandra dancing a Quadrille at Apsley House 1908. The end of an era.

Cheek to cheek

England 1919–1939

During the twenty years between the two world wars a few dozen Englishmen came nearer to reproducing the rhythms of the Greek tragic chorus in 5th-century B.C. Athens than anyone had, except a handful of Princes in the early Italian Renaissance.

They would have been very surprised had they been told this, for they believed that what they had been dancing was completely new, and that nothing like it had ever been done before. As to the high aesthetic value of their work, I don't suppose they ever gave it a thought. It was enough that they enjoyed dancing, and dancing this particular dance was its own reward.

For the dance was slow Foxtrot in the style and technique that had been formulated by the English in the 1920s. Several very different influences had coalesced.

By the Edwardian decade, at the beginning of this century, dancing in the West was becoming very tired. We had been waltzing for about a hundred years, and polkaing for sixty, all on our toes and with our feet turned out. We had been marching through Quadrille and the Lancers for the same amount of time, and galloping round the ballroom to Strauss. For the sake of variety many dancing-masters were reduced to making up little dances like the Military Twostep, in a style one might call 'chocolate soldier dancing'. There was also a languorous form of Tango that was considered very 'fast'.

What rescued us from this empty state of affairs was American ragtime. This has often been described as Negro rhythm combined with evangelistic hymn tune harmonies. Be that as it may, what concerns us is the vitality·of the 4/4 syncopated music. It was a rhythm you could walk to, but not anything like a Strauss march.

The dance to this rhythm had already been through various incarnations in America, most of them short-lived and usually dubbed with animal names, Bunny Hug, Turkey Trot and so on. Then just before the great war an Englishman called Vernon Castle and his American wife Irene, began dancing really beautifully to ragtime.

Had Vernon Castle not have been killed in the war he would probably have been the outstanding personality in ballroom dancing, and been able to dictate a technique decided by himself. As it was, English technique was the result of a

The Turkey Trot
One of various 'animal' dances, later to be tamed into the Foxtrot.

Post-war 1920s Tango. 'Punch' never changed his cruelty towards Modern Ballroom Dancing.

collaboration between most of the best ballroom dancers of the early twenties – a typically English process.

What emerged from this collaboration were four dances: slow Foxtrot, later known simply as Foxtrot; quick Foxtrot, later known as Quickstep; Waltz, a slow Waltz at about half the speed of the old Waltz; and Tango, a smooth, restrained Tango unlike both the pre-war Edwardian Tango and the staccato contortions we see today.

What basically they had to work on was (1) the old Waltz, now getting much slower. (A version of the Waltz called the Boston had in 1912 even tried to get our feet straight instead of turned out, and our heels down on the ground at certain points.) (2) The new 'walking' dances, all based on ragtime, in which the man walked forward and the girl for the most part walked backwards.

Before I continue I had better make something quite clear. The technique that emerged from all the arguments and compromises was learnt seriously by only a fraction of the population and, of that fraction, danced really well by only a few people. The great mass of the public just went on walking about, or only too often, waddling about. After the early 1920s it was the exception rather than the rule for the average person ever to have had proper dancing lessons. He thought ballroom dancing was something he picked up naturally, and that it really didn't matter much anyway. There were a few absolutely outstanding ballroom dancers of whom C. B. Fry, the cricketer, was one. Of these, quite a few, having won competitions and championships, turned professional and taught and demonstrated. They were a quite different type of person from the old pre-war type of dancing-master who had taught both ballroom dancing and a genteel

'Punch' at it again, this time with the Waltz.

form of ballet. It is ballroom dancing at this professional, or expert amateur level, that I shall be discussing here. Very few of the old film clips available today show anything but the untaught herds strolling or pushing about, so it is hard to believe just how different good ballroom dancing was.

The first aim was to get our feet parallel again. The turned out position had been *de rigueur* for so long that it was hard to convince people about the necessity for this. In 1924, the committee for the newly founded Ballroom Branch of the Imperial Society of Teachers of Dancing said that from now on parallel feet were to be the rule in social dancing.

This date exceeds by only one year the third centenary of our original evidence, that the feet were to be turned out (1623 de Lauze's Apologie de la Danse). A rule that had lasted for three hundred and one years was reversed at last.

Having at last got our feet parallel officially, we are faced with the second problem, how to vary the straightforward walking Foxtrot and manoeuvre the girl round the corners of the room.

⁂ They worked on the basis of the turns in the Waltz. These consist of three steps, 'forward, to the side and close' on which the man makes half a turn; and another three steps 'back, to the side and close' on which he makes another half turn. He finishes the whole turn facing in the same direction as when he started.

Each of these three step combinations was translated into 4/4 time to the rhythm slow, quick, quick, with the first step taken on the flat but rising on the balls of the feet for the side and close. This side step and close is called a chassé.

This remained the rule for Foxtrot when played at a quick tempo, fifty plus bars to the minute, which from now on we will call Quickstep.

At this tempo to make a turn on two chassé half turns proved difficult, and what developed was a figure called 'the quarter-turns' in which the men began the first half of a turn to the right but then took one step back and did the backward half of a turn to the left. This became the first basic step of Quickstep, just as the chassé became the characteristic of most of its turns.

Mechanically a chassé turn really is only a Waltz step done in duple time to an uneven rhythm. But when we come to slow Foxtrot we get something really new.

One of the essentials of really good Ballroom was that the front of the girl's body should be in such close contact with the front of the man's that they move completely as one, with one centre of gravity. Without this complete contact at the hips it is impossible to do slow Foxtrot at all. Foxtrot played at a tempo of thirty plus bars a minute seemed to need a more flowing movement than was attainable by the chassé turns of Quickstep. This was achieved by something quite new in my experience in the history of dancing: that is the heel turn for the girl.

Already the girl's technique in this dancing had showed some quite new features. That she should for the most part be moving backwards was new; in 19th-century Waltz, with its constant turns, she was turning forward as often as backwards. That she should be almost glued to the front of the man's hips was new; in old Waltz she was nothing like as close as this, and although they were moving in rhythm with each other they were still two distinct bodies. But now, in

Mannequin Parade at Lennards (1925) demonstrated by ballroom dancers, showing the restrained style beginning to come into professional work. Note the close contact between the dancers, necessary for the man to give a lead to all the steps.

terms of body mechanics, she does something which is quite brilliant and new. She provides, with her small, highish heels, a minute pivot point round which the man is able to turn a full 180°; not a closed Waltz turn with a chassé, but a turn with the third step carrying along down the line of dance instead of closing up to the second foot and punctuating the flow of their progress down the room.

This 'open turn' of the man's, giving an uninterrupted flow of movement, is the great characteristic of Foxtrot. It is possible only because of the girl's heel turns, and her close and stabilizing contact with him at the centre of his turning circle. When she is on the outer curve of their turn, and he has to provide a centre for her, not nearly such a large degree of turn is possible.

One other new thing in this technique is the long gliding steps they both make, skimming the heel along the floor. This step often rises at the end on to the ball of the foot, something that required a good deal of control and strength in the pelvis. Once the long glide with the rise is mastered we can really begin to dance Foxtrot; Slow Waltz and Quickstep are child's-play after that. (We will deal with Tango at the end.)

Having listed the new features in this technique we will now say what is old in it. The rise and fall are as old as the early Italian Renaissance (Aiere and Movimento). The Contra-body movement, essential for all these turns, is similarly from the Quattrocento and indeed is the first time we get full Maniera again since we went into farthingales and padded doublets. Finally, the rhythms of Foxtrot are pure Greek. Slow, slow, quick, quick, slow – those spondees and anapaests again. ✳

In view of the extreme beauty of these dances, certainly slow Foxtrot and slow Waltz, why were they not acclaimed as the artistic achievements which in many performances I have seen they undoubtedly were? This was due to one of those unfortunate accidents that happen in this life.

It will be easily understood that this technique requires a certain amount of space for its performance. Not that, like the Danse à Deux, the couple require the whole dancing floor for themselves. But it is not possible to do Foxtrot in a small room.

The 1920s saw a great change in our social habits in London. Many of the old great houses were pulled down and fewer private balls were given. Going out to dinner and dance in restaurants and hotels became quite permissible, indeed fashionable, and even more so, going on to a night-club after the theatre to have supper and dance into the small hours. Most of these places had very good bands.

What they notably lacked were large dance floors. West End rents were rising astronomically and very often the more fashionable the night-club the smaller was the available space. This meant that serious ballroom dancing was not able to be done there. Where there *was* space, and where good ballroom dancing began to be seen more and more, was at the dance-halls in the suburbs.

We have mentioned already as a fact of life that, if something associated with an admired set of people is taken by up an unadmired set, then it is dropped very quickly by the first group. Modern ballroom had, to start with, been popularized by very distinguished people, the then Prince of Wales among them. By the middle of the 1930s, when the old class structure in this country had not yet totally disappeared, to become suburban in this way meant social death. Serious

modern Ballroom was in fact on the way to becoming the cult activity it now is.

An added complication was in the music. The two official forms of Foxtrot, Quickstep and slow Foxtrot, required tempi about fifty plus and thirty plus bars a minute respectively. In the dance-halls these tempi were maintained, though not with the deadly metronome regularity they are today. On the other hand, these bands were usually run-of-the-mill combinations. The really good and much admired West End dance-bands were laws unto themselves. Carroll Gibbons at the Savoy, Ambrose at the Mayfair, Roy Fox and Lew Stone played their 4/4 music at a tempo they felt best suited it and best suited their customers, who for the most part just strolled rhythmically about the floor. Very often the best tempo for this was just between slow Foxtrot and Quickstep and not suitable for either. The Ballroom Branch of the Imperial Society tried to make a special new dance for this tempo (it was called the midway rhythm) but it never got off the ground. All this was one more nail in the coffin.

But the last of our four dances perhaps had the greatest influence on the general view of ballroom as socially a 'good thing' or not. Tango was in its mechanics the odd man out. The steps were not glided but walked. There was no rise and fall; it is a flat dance. There is no normal Contra-body movement in Tango for the torso is in a permanent oblique position in relation to the legs: the

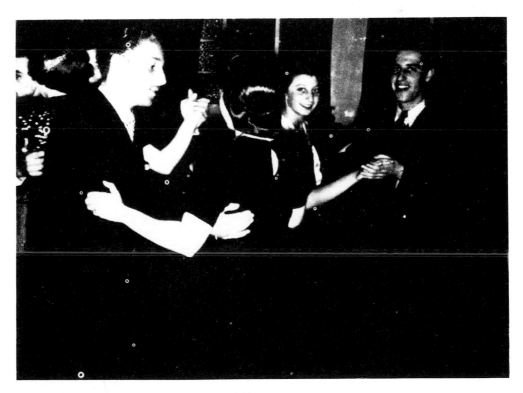

Ballroom in the dance hall, Whitechapel 1938.

Left: Henry Jacques and Miss Allen. The English style of ballroom dancing at its best.

right shoulder and side of the body is forward, and the legs and feet are at an angle to this, the feet not closing level with each other as in Foxtrot and Waltz, but one a little behind the other.

But it was not the mechanics of Tango, slinky as they were, that gave it its sultry reputation. One of the great romantic figures of the twenties had been the filmstar Rudolph Valentino. In the film The Four Horsemen of the Apocalypse he had danced a wonderful Tango. He was a magnificent dancer. Now at any age to have as a partner a man who dances badly must always have been irritating, but until we come to modern ballroom this was not totally incapacitating. One could still dance well oneself. With old Waltz it must have been touch and go, but with modern ballroom it became impossible. The girl cannot dance any better than the man she is dancing with; she can only help him to dance his best. In the 1920s the change to a totally new deportment and style left many middle-aged men in the world of Waltz, and unwilling to learn new tricks. Many of their middle-aged wives, on the other hand, had taken to the new style. There was therefore a demand for good partners and this was supplied by many professionals.

As a rule these were very pleasant men and nearly all the ones I knew I liked very much. But to the normal English male they were simply gigolos. 'Damn dagos', was the usual condemnation, for the dark ones at least. (A very good picture of this attitude is given in Dorothy L. Sayers's, Have His Carcase.)

There were in fact two totally contrasted images of Ballroom dancing in the public's mind in the 1920s and 1930s. One was the seductive Latin male, dancing a Tango with Tarquin's ravishing strides. This was the socially unacceptable one; the inscrutable Valentino glowed and sulked behind it. The other image couldn't have been more different: fair, slim, lightish, with facets of Bertie Wooster and Lord Peter Wimsey; dancing a little Quickstep or Foxtrot with complete insouciance and great good humour: in the person of His Royal Highness the Prince of Wales, Mr Jack Buchanan or the one and only Fred Astaire.

Let's Twist again

Doing Our Own Thing

1939–1976

One of the things which had made Foxtrot so beautiful was the long flowing dresses that the girls wore when they were demonstrating. These were usually made of silk chiffon, in subtle pastel or clear jewel colours, and they flowed round their feet emphasizing the fluid curves of the dance. Never a spangle was in sight.

With the outbreak of the second world war French silk chiffon became unattainable. Hard on the heels of this came clothes rationing. One of the few materials that were not rationed was net. In those days it was rayon net but it was very similar to the nylon net of today. Net does not hang and flow like silk chiffon and if a skirt made of net is to be wide enough to dance in, then, perforce, it must be somewhat bouffant in style.

The trouble here was that the style of the movement in good Ballroom does not suit a bouffant dress. It cuts the line of the leg and the back and ruins the whole flow of the dance. I think it is very sad to see what effect this type of dress has had on the actual dancing. The old simplicity and flow seem to be no longer admired, and I sometimes wonder whether most competition dancers wouldn't be happier if they were trying to do some sort of ballet. The whole of English modern Ballroom dancing, however, has nothing to do with social dancing now. It is a specialist cult followed by its own devotees, and they and their friends enjoy it greatly. It includes the four main dances, Foxtrot, Quickstep, Waltz and Tango; formation dancing, which was first seen in the thirties, and which can be very interesting, but so often looks as if it were being performed by automatons. And very popular, in this specialist world, the Latin-American dances, Rumba, Samba, Cha-Cha-Cha, and Pasodoblé. Here the ornateness of the costumes knows no bounds, but I feel that each of these dances should be a cabaret number by itself, with the audience watching a single couple. There should not be several on the floor together and not in a competitive situation.

What happened to cause this parting of the ways was that when our American allies came over here in the last war they brought their Jitterbugging with them. Dancing was the great popular diversion in the war, and all the army and R.A.F. camps throughout the country held regular dances. Prior to the American influx, these had tended to be staid. Uniformed couples, clasped warmly in each other's arms, perambulated together around the floor, with an occasional Lambeth Walk to liven things up. This was a processional dance, popularized by Lupino Lane in the show Me and My Girl. It had a very slight mimetic element.

The Americans soon put an end to any stodginess. We have never looked back since. From Jitterbug to Jive, from Jive to Rock-and-Roll, from Rock-and-Roll to the Twist, and from then on to the more recherché items of Afro-American culture it has all been one way traffic.

The really interesting thing about this post-war period is the development of the music, and as this is being dealt with separately, all I need do here is to point out the main mechanical features and how they reflect or compare with the last eight hundred and fifty years of our Western culture.

Jitterbug greatly increased the dynamic range of our social dancing. Some of the movements were very strong, indeed rough – the man pulling the girl towards him with one hand, and then twisting her round under his arm and then away again. But the important thing was the departure from the close, old Ballroom hold to dancing with one's partner at arm's length.

Energetic Jitterbugs at the New York World's Fair.

This was only a transitional stage to the complete separation of the partners, and this has remained the norm for most of the time since. When Bing Crosby was being interviewed by Michael Parkinson in 1975, he sang a little song about wanting to hold the girl when he was dancing, and 'not the empty air'. He and Michael Parkinson agreed that from their point of view the recent developments were a great pity. 'They don't even touch each other,' said Bing, 'they'll be phoning in next.'

As far as body mechanics go, the important thing is the different use of the foot and of the pelvis. The latter change has been seen most obviously in the Twist, but it has been there from the start of Jitterbugging.

As I have said before we have always taken our dance rhythms from a primitive level of society, where the creative impulse has not been inhibited by our critical faculties. We took these rhythms first from our own peasantry, then from Germany and Eastern Europe, then from the Black culture in the States, and from our West Indian immigrants. From the Renaissance, right up to the beginning of the last war, we all did one thing for certain when we took any peasant movement into Polite Society. We stabilized the pelvis. Unless our hip girdle is held in a strong muscular grip we have not the central stability to rise and sink on our feet with ease and control. This may have been temporarily neglected in the 'tippy-toe' period of the 19th century, but it was returned to with great emphasis in the inter-war period of good modern Ballroom. But since the last war the pelvis, in popular dancing, has been positively vagrant.

I think there are two unfortunate things about letting the hip girdle go like this. First, though it looks beautiful done by Blacks, it does not look good when done by Whites. (There are a few exceptions.) We aren't built to make movements like that; our torsos haven't that kind of fluidity.

Secondly, by failing in this central control we are unable to use our feet economically. For much of the time we leave them quite flaccidly on the floor, and make all the rhythmic accents with our hips. This necessitates slack knees as well.

The progressive desensitization and misuse of the Western foot is disturbing I think. The elastic precision of which our feet are capable is a feature which the late Dr Bronowski would have listed under 'human specificity'. It is one of our characteristic differences from the apes. They cannot achieve our swinging walk, and can only toddle, and waddle, and slouch.

It is not just in social dancing that we are neglecting our feet. In physical education the increasing popularity of the trampoline is ominous. In trampolining the long arch of the foot is flattened out by the concavity of the canvas surface, as we rely on a piece of external apparatus to supply the spring we no longer make ourselves. Again there is an excessive use of bent knees.

In both these activities the foot is rather like a dead fish. But the opposite, a stiffened, hard foot, is just as bad. Because of the peculiar shoes they employ we tend to get this rigid foot both in ballet and in Ballroom. The blocked toe is obviously absurd from the point of view of rational mechanics, but really no more wasteful than the high heel of the girl's shoe in Ballroom. They both ruin the natural leverage of the foot; we wouldn't dream of treating our car springs like that.

The wear and tear to our bodies would be greatly reduced if we restored this natural shock absorbing quality to our feet. I will, of course, be accused of wanting to take us back to a past that is gone. W. H. Auden said:

We know no fuss or pain or lying
can stop the moribund from dying,
that all the special tasks begun
by the Renaissance have been done.

The point is that I don't think the special tasks of the Renaissance are nearly done yet. If one of them is to make us as reasonable about our own body mechanics as we would be about any other machine, then most of it is still to do.

'(Baby), save the last dance for me . . .'

Rock 'n' roll was pop music: music of the people. And also dance music. The man who dreamt up the term, Alan Freed, was a classical disc jockey in Cleveland Ohio who was fascinated by the way kids moved to the records he heard at local music stores and dance halls. No one had told him all this was going on. And the stars of Dick Clark's TV show *American Bandstand*, which helped to start a craze for rock 'n' roll across the States, were not the men who made the records but the 150 kids from the Philadelphia streets who came into the studio to dance to them.

As popular music rock 'n' roll had something to say about the way society was changing. Young people didn't want to be like their parents any more. They wanted to shake off the strict Fifties attitude to sex: the Great American Repression. And the inspiration? That was hardly a topic for intense debate, at least in those days. But Alan Freed had been among the first to comment on the fact that the new dance and music of white American youth flowed from an alien culture.

After the war, Negro jazz musicians, influenced by Charlie Parker, had abandoned regular rhythms. 'Bop' or 'cool' jazz wasn't dance music. But the dance music tradition remained in the northern cities, like Chicago's South Side: small bands used electric guitars to amplify a heavy beat still based on the old blues. There were all kinds of different Negro dance music – the Chicago blues, big bands, gospel sounds. Altogether they were called, loosely, 'rhythm and blues'.

Alan Freed started playing Negro music to white audiences, but before long white bands were also trying to cater for the taste for uptempo four-beats-to-the-bar songs at dance halls. People like Bill Haley, Carl Perkins, and later Elvis

Presley sang a rhythm and blues coloured by the more familiar sound of white country music. The sound was an instant success, and the new network of electronic media – TV, juke boxes, radio – helped the craze sweep right across the States. And then to Britain. Soon Hollywood movies followed the records, and British teenagers caught onto the dance as well as the music. If dance was what you called it.

Many people wouldn't. They were too shocked. As rock 'n' roll lyrics had nothing to do with the oblique clichés of Eddie Fisher or Dickie Valentine or even Sinatra, so the dance was worlds apart from the ballroom dancing of the British Palais: even the cha-cha.

But rock 'n' roll dancing, or jiving, wasn't really so new. On both sides of the Atlantic jiving was based on the jitterbug, whose roots were in the Jazz Age dances like the Charleston and the Black Bottom. In those days, at Gatsby's parties for example, couples would throw themselves (or each other) around in a rough imitation of sexual frenzy, parting their legs or moving their breasts as they thought Negroes might have done in the Deep South if they'd had enough moonshine whisky. At least one newspaper said it was a Bolshevik conspiracy.

The jitterbug, popular in the Forties, was just as frenetic at first, but its more hysterical aspect was soon contained by the strict tempos and taut arrangements of the Big Bands. It was a casual, improvised dance, far from the close embrace of the Waltz; couples moved together only to move away again and touch fingertips, one leg akimbo. Jitterbugging was called jiving in its last days. American servicemen helped to make it popular in Britain.

Rock 'n' roll was similar but more overtly sexual. The count was a simple one, one, two, one, two, in line with the pounding beat, and there was no rule about which partner should use which foot at any one time. It was hard to tell who was leading; it could be either the man or the girl and sometimes it didn't matter at all. But it was still alright to throw your partner around in a manner that simulated the most athletic kind of sex. The girl would throw her legs around the man's waist, lean back and open her legs, and the two would swirl around each other (or over, or under), fingertips clutched and arms outstretched. The centre of gravity, as Elvis Presley ('the Pelvis') showed everyone, was definitively sexual. The whole performance was such a direct imitation of sex it may have been a substitute rather than a form of seduction; but sexology is a recent art and that must remain speculative.

Not surprisingly, rock 'n' roll was widely condemned as the entertainment of degenerates, a kinetic version of those oriental drugs that were said to drive men to sexual abuse and homicide. Serious people argued that rock 'n' roll was not just a symptom. It might also be a disease that would destroy the Constitution. White kids were starting to act like Negroes. Things were falling apart.

There was some truth in this. Something new was happening: *teenagers*. As the rock 'n' roll boom began. James Dean was busy creating the teenage persona for the first time in *Rebel Without a Cause*: moody, sexy, thoughtful, violent in a way that only seemed random to the outsider. The Misunderstood. Brando had already popularized a mood of smouldering rebellion. And writers like Jack Kerouac and Allen Ginsberg (who first read *Howl* the month Dean died) extended the spirit of revolt onto the campus. Or even into the intellectual class-

Elvis Presley, whose erotic pelvic gyrations symbolized the new teenage property, Rock 'n' Roll.

room. Mick Jagger's neighbour in class used to read Kerouac's *On the Road* behind his text books.

Rock 'n' roll dance was different from the Jazz Age dances because it was part of a more general revolt that could only end up with a political character. The seeds of teenage rebellion were firmly trampled on in the Fifties as rock 'n' roll became commercialized, an in-built part of the Establishment. But there was now a precedent, a kind of inspiration.

Rock 'n' roll in Britain was a form of popular rebellion in a way that many later pop trends were not. It had a genuine social base: the dance halls, the coffee bars with their Sieberg juke boxes and Gaggia espresso machines, anywhere teenagers could meet beyond the eyes of their parents. Or the law. Even street corners would do. Rock 'n' roll was soon a visible form of delinquency. It couldn't be confined to the dance hall –

'The queue outside the Palais was large but quite orderly. . . . Unlike most of the films, this one had commanded an almost entirely adolescent audience. When the music started it was infectious – no one managed to keep still. It was the first time the gangs had been exposed to an animal rhythm that matched their behaviour. Soon couples were in the aisles copying the jiving on the screen. . . . The audience went mad. . . .' (Rock Around the Clock, Sep. '56.)

If you couldn't dance for the seats, rip the seats out. The motto of the rock culture of the Fifties and Sixties.

If rock 'n' roll was an attack, maybe violent, on the established entertainment industry, it was also a native phenomenon that took its *form* from the States. The new dance had local roots. There were Teddy Boys before Elvis. British rock 'n' roll fans developed a distinctive style – drainpipe trousers, greased hair, long jackets, luminous socks – that indirectly imitated the white New York street gangs; but then those gangs were in turn imitations of the Negro kids in Harlem in the Forties.

Britain had its own rock 'n' roll stars too. At first singers like Tommy Steele and Cliff Richard (really Tommy Hicks, Harry Webb) were 'discovered' by impresarios in the Soho coffee bars. Later, as this spontaneity of the rock 'n' roll boom grew cold, the British stars were merely local imitations of Elvis: Marty Wilde, Billy Fury, or Terry Dene, who spoilt the image by cracking up and crying off-stage. In the States too the gold lamé was wearing thin by the end of the Fifties. Record companies were turning out new stars like a Detroit assembly line: Fabian, Frankie Avalon. As for Elvis: once shown on TV only from the waist upwards, he'd since joined the Army, and gone soft.

Not only did the new stars lack roots in any sub-culture (except maybe Dion, Neil Sedaka), they lacked *style*. Style was the way rock 'n' roll culture expressed itself. It meant dance, music, clothes, the way you moved, and it could turn everyday things into objects of adoration. *You can do anything, but don't tread on my blue suede shoes,* sang Carl Perkins. Rock 'n' roll fans in Kenneth Anger's films caress their cars and motor-bikes as if they were sexual objects. They were.

As the style faded, so did the dance. The first two years of the Sixties were a bleak moment in the history of pop culture. Everyone wanted something new, and so the entertainment industry found something new to give them. The Twist.

The Twist was a song, and a dance. The song, just called 'The Twist', was originally the flipside of an American hit by Hank Ballard in 1959. A year later it was recorded by Ernest Evans, once a chicken plucker, and now a singer called Chubby Checker, who performed the song and the dance you did to it on *American Bandstand*. There was nothing special about the record, it was just a kind of pallid rock 'n' roll, like all the later 'Twist' hits. Sometimes old rock 'n' roll records were even re-released, undoctored, as Twist songs, as the craze gathered speed in the States in '61 and in Britain in '62.

The dance was something else. No one's sure where it came from, although the dance expert Frances Rust suggests it's a stylized version of the way rock 'n' roll

Birmingham schoolchildren 'rocking' to the sound of a juke box (1957), showing the typical 'hunched up' male position with weight forward on the toes.

Right: Chubby Checker demonstrating 'The Twist' with two English dance teachers.

singers swung their hips. It was very simple. All you had to do was move your feet as if you were trying to stub out a cigarette you'd dropped on the dance hall floor, and you moved your hips as if you were drying the sweat off your back with a towel.

Richard Mabey (*'The Pop Process'*) quotes the words of Manhattan dance instructor Killer Joe Piro in the *Saturday Evening Post*:

'All that hip movement. . . . It's got new names, but you know they were doing that at the Savoy Ballroom in Harlem when I was 17. Remember that boogie-woogie shuffle that Cab Calloway used to do? Harlem was doing the Twist 30

years ago and didn't know it. Negroes and teenagers, that's where the new dances come from. . . . I watch them and I steal a lot of their stuff. Sometimes I have to clean it up.'

Killer Joe was teaching the Twist to adults. Adults liked it because it was simple and you could clean it up easily enough. Teenagers liked it because it could be sexy and it was a simple affair to find a new partner. As in the days of Elvis the Pelvis, the centre of gravity was still in the hips, but you could move your hips very discreetly indeed. In fact you didn't have to do very much at all. If you worked up a sweat it was as likely to be in an effort to slim as simulate sex. Chubby Checker proved that himself, losing 35 lbs in the first year of the Twist.

The Twist was also a safe dance. Stubbing out that cigarette was symbolic. No dance halls got wrecked. In Britain the Mecca and other chains were even responsible for promoting it, right from the start. (You could, of course, fit more people onto the dance floor!) There's no doubt the Twist was a commercial affair. Everyone was cashing in from the moment it started. They didn't wait for the craze to sober down, as they'd done in '56. Dance schools offered Twist classes. One firm sold 15,000 pairs of Twist shoes in a fortnight. 'Doing the Twist', a paperback, sold 125,000 copies in ten days.

The Twist was the first hint that a teenage culture could affect adults too. And it cut across the class as well as the age barrier. It was the first symptom of what Tom Wolfe later called *radical chic*: the appropriation of teenage subculture imagery by the rich and fashionable and reasonably intellectual. Brigitte Bardot did it. Jackie Kennedy denied doing it but not everyone believed her. One of the first Twist hits was Joey Dee and the Starlighters *Peppermint Twist*, which started climbing the British charts in January '62, the same month as *The Twist*. Joey Dee played nightly at New York's Peppermint Lounge, a night resort for the city's older hipsters. And that was the kind of place the Twist began. Not just in dance halls.

The Twist was a foretaste of changes in society. But it was crucial in the history of dance. After the Waltz people had started dancing in couples rather than in groups. After the Twist, they were happy to dance alone. It was the first kind of popular dance in which you didn't touch your partner. You didn't even need a partner. Nor did you have to learn any steps. Anyone could do it.

Of course you could learn how to do it better. There were always minor variations you could throw in. If you didn't go to a dance class, you perfected these in front of a mirror. Sometimes it dawned on people: the bedroom rehearsal was as much a real dance as the Twist session at the party later. You danced with your own reflection. The Twist was a way of doing your own thing and being part of a group at the same time. More cynically, it was also the start of popular dance as a form of narcissism.

A flood of other dances followed the Twist; the Madison, the Mashed Potato (stamp your feet and mash imaginary spuds), the Blues (hands behind your (back), the Turkey Trot (flap your elbows like wings, reflections of Ragtime?), the Marilyn (a parody of Marilyn Monroe's walk), the Penguin Bounce, the Robot, the Dog. They all made it and then faded away quickly. Finally everyone was doing their own dance. In the next decade, from '65 to '75, there were only three exceptions: black kids, Mods, and hippies.

A Twist lesson in progress showing the basic foot and body movements, and hinting at the narcissistic quality of the new solo dance form.

As rock 'n' roll declined, British pop musicians – the real musicians, not the manufactured stars – began to look back to the roots of the music. Already in the late Fifties Lonnie Donegan had scored a string of Top Ten hits with *skiffle* music. He'd been listening to black blues singers like Leadbelly and Lonnie Johnson (who unwittingly loaned his name to Tony Donnegan), and white folk singers like Woody Guthrie. Donegan just added a fast dance beat and then showed everyone how to play the music themselves. All you needed was a string bass (tea chest, broom handle), a drum (washboard), a guitar, and any kind of voice, and you had a skiffle group. Donegan showed British pop fans how they could make their own dance music instead of merely dropping the latest American hit onto the record player. Already some amateur groups were using electric guitars, and imitating the slick professional sounds of people like The Shadows, Cliff Richard's backing group.

The American musicians Donegan copied often sang music with a message: social, political, as well as sexual. Many young people in Britain who were interested in radical change began listening to their music too. And so began the liaison between popular music and politics that later formed a *rock culture*. It was, unlike rock 'n' roll, an articulate and self-conscious protest that depended on *content* as well as *form*. Style was still important. But, as the rock 'n' roll age ended, style was no longer the unique constituent of youthful rebellion. The long-haired Beatniks, for example, expressed their contempt for conventional society in their life-style (i.e. dress, jobs, or lack of jobs, slang, music); but the Beats who went on the CND nuclear disarmament marches also had a very definite message to put across. As the importance of style declined, dance started to lose its central position in the youth culture.

At first Donegan sang in Chris Barber's band. Barber, like Ken Colyer and Humphrey Lyttelton, played 'Traditional' jazz – a British version of the New Orleans dance bands. Their sound was dominated by reed instruments (like Kenny Ball's clarinet) and banjos. Suddenly, for no apparent reason, their music stopped being a minority cult and started making the Hit Parade. Some people had been dancing to Trad for years. Rock critic Dick Gilbert recalls a Trad night at Oxford University's Jazz Club in '58:

'Most people went along to dance. You'd ask someone to dance and hope they knew the steps. If they didn't, you'd have to explain. You'd say: "Look, I'm going to do a skip-jive, ok?" And you'd have to say whether you were going to do it slow time or double time to the beat. Some people there were really famous for dancing. If you were looking at anyone else, it was more likely to be a couple dancing than the band.'

The Trad boom didn't last long. Many fans soon got bored of the bands' Mickey-Mouse qualities, their tweed suits and glib manner, and the stiff banjo rhythms didn't seem so much fun to dance to after all. Instead they turned their attention to another kind of black music: rhythm and blues. They didn't have to look far. The Chris Barber Band was playing R&B as well as Trad. 'R&B,' says Dick Gilbert, 'was something totally new.'

By now R&B had a fairly specific meaning: it was the blues music of the big cities in the northern states of the US, especially Chicago. It was played most often with a small band – bass, piano, drums, harmonica, electric guitar – and it was a rough, raucous, heavily amplified sound with a very strong beat. The top R&B musicians were men like Big Bill Broonzy, Sonny Boy Williamson, Muddy Waters. In '57 Muddy played on tour with the Barber Band. His electric and sexy stage manner inspired people like Alexis Korner, a member of Barber's band who later formed his own group: *Blues Incorporated*.

Blues Inc was the most important London band of the early Sixties. John Mayall, Graham Bond, and Long John Baldry worked with Korner and then spread the word to friends like Eric Clapton, Ginger Baker, Jack Bruce, Rod Stewart. Mick Jagger, Keith Richard, and Charlie Watts also played with Korner. One night Korner was supposed to be playing at London's Marquee Club, but he also had a recording date at the BBC. The BBC, says Korner, couldn't afford all the musicians so the second vocalist filled in at the Marquee with some friends: the Rolling Stones.

The earliest fans of R&B were some of the more trendy young London aristocrats, who'd already turned onto the Twist and now wanted something less banal at their balls and parties, and the young folk club fans, many of them left-wing or Young Communists. It seems an odd mixture, but both groups were trying to create an identity remote from what they saw as the middle-class and suburban conformity of the Macmillan era (the Profumo scandal and the Wilson administration were yet to come).

Neither group had much interest in developing any special kind of R&B dance. For the club fans the music was too serious, and for the others it was too peripheral to their lives, only a sideshow. For R&B fans, dance, performers, and music were all equally important. The Beatles changed all that. They were stars. And as Flick Colby, director of the *Top of the Pop's* Pan's People, says: 'You can't dance to the Beatles.'

In the early Sixties there were many local dance groups around the Mersey who imitated the strong beat of the Shadows. They were influenced, too, by the American harmony singing of the Everly Brothers, and more recently The Four Seasons; and by the early soul sounds of black American groups like the Shirelles. Many of these records were brought over by the American sailors and their British workmates, the 'Cunard Yanks' who docked in Liverpool with the latest American hits. Since many other people were out of work, there were dozens of eager groups who copied the American sounds in the nasal local accent, hoping to find a way out of the Merseyside depression. There were also plenty of people with time to spend at the city's main club, the Cavern.

People went to listen to the music. The Merseybeat was a new sound, literally *electric*. Groups like the Escorts, the Tremeloes . . . and the Beatles . . . turned the bass volume amplifiers up and used drums, rhythm and bass guitars to create a heavy accentuated beat. It was *loud*. Almost a wall of sound. You didn't really dance to the music. You just moved. Richard Mabey remembers:

'*The couples are dancing again, most of them standing quite still facing each other, whilst they twitch and jerk their arms and heads. This seems to be partly an imitation of the rhythmic movements that guitarists unconsciously make as they are playing, and partly a simple solution of the problem of how to dance when it is too crowded to move.*'

The Beatles and other Mersey groups began to dominate the national Hit Parade in late '63, and the London R&B groups like the Stones made just enough compromise with the new sound to break into the charts themselves. 'We'll be happy,' said the Beatles, 'if we last as long as Cliff and the Shadows.' But by late '64 it was clear something very different was going on. The Beatles and the Stones didn't change, as Cliff had done, to fit the conventions of society and the media. They were starting to create a new culture.

The media spread the words and deeds of the new groups around the country far more efficiently than they'd ever done in the days of rock 'n' roll. Kids who copied the Stones and Beatles had a whole range of new trends to choose from, and dance was one of the least important. The new culture was also happy to express itself directly. The Beatles, said John Lennon, are more popular than Jesus. There was less need now for the *indirect* expression of dance.

There were other reasons why the amazing success of the Beatles was never accompanied by a distinctive dance style. The advent of electronic media – tapes, car radios, transistors, cheaper TV – meant you could enjoy the new sounds in your own home. You didn't have to go to a dance hall. If you did, there was every chance you'd stand on the seats and scream instead of dancing – even if you were a boy, you'd sit and stare. It was the performer that mattered. Sometimes the screaming was so intense, no-one heard the music, not even the group. Finally, even if you did dance, there was a whole gallery of subdued styles to choose from. TV shows like *Ready Steady Go* and *Top of the Pops* had made all kinds of dancing acceptable. Dance styles had diffused, often to a point where you could hardly see them.

Richard Mabey again:

'Up near the stage are a group of girls aged between twelve and fourteen. . . . Scattered around the hall are clusters of boys in a curious aggressive stance: heads thrust forward, backs arched like longbows, arms folded in front of their bodies. They will gaze at the girls but rarely ask them to dance. Occasionally one will burst into rapid movement, then, dissatisfied, lope off to a new station on the floor. Simultaneously three or four others will rise up like a flock of birds and follow him.

In one corner, a group of rockers from a nearby village have linked arms and are doing high-kicks so energetically that you can hear the stamping of their motor-cycle boots above the music. The few country girls in their costumes and flared dresses are still doing the Twist, but that jerky dance from Merseyside has reached the South, and most of the girls are twitching their arms and heads in little groups of threes and fours. The boys, too, seem more willing to do this dance – which most people round here call the Shake or the Robot – than the more extravagant and potentially embarrassing movements of the Twist.'

That's from a description of a dance at the Town Hall at Berkhamsted, Hertfordshire, in December '63. As Mabey points out, local dances were easier to finance after the wave of Beatlemania. But there's no doubt the centre of the Swinging Sixties was London: *Swinging London*, as Time Magazine called it. The styles of revolt promoted casually by the Beatles and more aggressively by the Stones were soon extended – for love or money – by young people working in film, theatre, fashion, design, photography.

The Sixties pop culture also learnt from the Mods. The Beatles and the Stones went Mod for a time, and The Who were a definitive Mod band – stripes, sharp, short jackets, Union Jacket waistcoats. As seen by rock stars and artists, the Mod style was close to the Pop Art of Andy Warhol: surface style meant everything, content nothing. It was the medium that mattered (to re-apply the famous line of Marshall McLuhan), not the message. This was closer to the spirit of rock 'n' roll, and the spirit of dance. And it was the Mods, and the black kids they danced with, who first revived popular dance in the Sixties.

The Mods were mainly southern city kids. They had regular seaside fights with the Rockers, who they saw as greasy louts embedded in a long-dead tradition of rock 'n' roll. The Rockers thought the Mods were sickly, neurotic, effete. They didn't like the clothes the Mods bought in Carnaby Street. And they didn't like the dances they learnt in discos with black kids: Ska, Blue Beat, Rock Steady.

Ska or Blue Beat, as it became known in Britain, began in the shanty towns of Jamaica around 1958. Its origins were in American R&B and the local religious cult of 'Pocomania'. A couple of years later young Jamaicans were dancing Ska in the clubs of Soho and Brixton. The Mods picked up the dance and in 1964 a young Jamaican girl called Millie made Blue Beat popular nationally with a hit song called *Lollipop*. The craze didn't last long, but it had a lasting influence on popular dancing in Britain.

Ska music meant a fast, monotonous rhythm and a heavily accented off-beat. Melody and lyrics were far less important. As for the dance, Frances Rust quotes the Jamaican band leader Ezz Rico:

'Imagine you have a terrible tummy-ache and a twitch at the same time. You've just got to move around to relieve the pain – well, man, that's blue beat. It may look like you're suffering, but the truth is, you're having a whole heap of fun.'

Orlando Patterson is more specific:

'The dancer stands with his feet slightly apart and his body bent from the waist, as in a bow. The body is then straightened out and bowed to the rhythm of the tune, the neck plunging in and out like a turkey. There are several hand movements, the most characteristic being a muscular jerk convulsing the whole body. It is carried out with the arms held out in front of the dancer, slightly bent at the elbows. The movements of the legs tend to vary with each performer.'

As in the Twist, there was no distinct role for the man or the girl, although most people still danced in couples. There were no distinct steps either, and since the dance involved the whole body there was more opportunity to improvise and be individual. And soon after the Blue Beat came 'The Shake', a far more ill-defined dance, a kind of lazy amalgam of the Twist and the Blue Beat: all you did was stand opposite your partner and shake your body as if you were standing on a vibrating platform. After that you could do anything.

And most people did. The Blue Beat was a specific, British craze. At the same time, in the States, the independent black record producer Berry Gordy had isolated the rhythmic component of black American dance music and added strings, a gospel style of singing, and smooth, bland voices to create just the kind of music you could do any dance to. Some of the artists on Gordy's Tamla Motown label were genuinely original: Smokey Robinson, Marvin Gaye. Others were simply manufactured 'soul' music intended for instant consumption in the new 'discotheques'.

The first 'disco' was in Paris. The idea was simple: a small, dark dance-hall, most often in a basement, run by people who were part of the same culture as the kids who went there. The music was likely to be soul and post-Beatles British rock, perhaps with a live band. They were a big city affair where strangers could meet, rather than a neighbourhood club. The new British discos could hardly be a stronger contrast to the typical draughty Palais of the Fifties.

Black kids in discos were still likely to dance a special style: passing, individual fashions, but most discos were for whites, and even if there was room to show off, few had the desire, or the ability. Nowadays strange, new, or extravagant dances were for strange, extravagant people: pop stars.

The two most salient, by far, are Mick Jagger and Tina Turner. Jagger's manner is well enough known: pouting, affected, wrist inverted on hip, arrogant, strutting around the stage, he contrives to be aggressively sexual and effeminate at the same time: only by being one can he get away with being the other. Today a simple display of *machismo* would attract as much laughter as a series of homo-

The high stepping Mick Jagger, arousing teenagers to emotional frenzy.

sexual postures. As Jagger became more and more theatrical in the late Sixties, styles of sex on the dance floor began not only to meet but to overlap.

There was sexual confusion too in the wild hysteria of black singer Tina Turner. She came on with a direct sexuality associated in the past only with male stars like Elvis Presley. And she made Elvis look like a pallid adolescent. Flashing around the stage in see-through dresses cut high above the knee, she'd throw her long hair and long limbs around as if she'd been plugged into an electric guitar lead. Nick Cohn's is the definitive description:

'So Tina started whirling and pounding and screaming, melting by the minute, and suddenly she came thundering down on me like an avalanche, backside first, all that flesh shaking and leaping in my face. And I reared back in self-defence, all the front rows did, and then someone fell over and we all immediately collapsed in a heap, struggling and cursing, thrashing about like a fish in a bucket.

When I looked up again, Tina was still shaking above us, her butt was still exploding, and she looked down on us in triumph. . . . She ate us all for breakfast.'

And all the time her husband, Ike Turner, would brood on his guitar in the background like a sulky chorus girl. Tina made men feel the way Mick Jagger made girls feel.

They both changed the way people danced. It wasn't just that the sexes were melting into each other. They both *performed*. 'I can teach you a thing or two about *performance*,' says Mick Jagger in the film of that name. Dancing became a way of displaying yourself. At best it was a kind of self-expression. At worst it was a mild form of narcissism, like dancing the Twist in front of a see-through mirror.

The new discos and TV shows like *Top of the Pops* began a fashion for solo girl dancers who performed for money: Go-Go dancers. Alice Richard, one of the first, remembers:

'It was a Sixties floor show, like Charleston girls without the upper-class overtones. There were set routines, but you could pick them up anywhere. You could still pick up some of the steps from the cha-cha. But most of the sexy wiggles and so on were just formalized versions of what everyone was doing on the dance floor.'

But the *flower power* culture of '67 made dancing solo intellectually respectable. The kind of dancing you could see at 'underground' clubs like the Middle Earth in Covent Garden and the UFO in Tottenham Court Road in '67 and '68 was the last distinctive style of dance to be associated with popular white culture. So far there hasn't been another.

At first it seemed that nothing could be less danceable than the music of the new culture. It was the *words* that mattered, and sometimes the *sound*. Pure rhythm was suddenly way down on the list. In late '66 the Beatles themselves, influenced by lysergic acid – LSD – recorded their *Sergeant Pepper* album. You could still dance to it, but it was the first album you were most likely to sit down and listen to, maybe for hours. Meanwhile in the States Bob Dylan, once a folk poet and protest singer, had taken a cue from the new British groups and started using an electric guitar. Sometimes you could dance to his music too, but after Dylan rock music was really a serious affair, like all the other art forms, and mere *dance* music seemed a thoroughly laughable concept. But the new culture was also trying to escape from words. Print culture, explained Marshall McLuhan, was dying. The 'underground' culture of the late Sixties rejected the Western method of dealing with reality by translating it into words. Words were a game, and a game you didn't have to play. Pictures, films, music, dance, no longer had to represent reality directly, and if they tried to, the effect was more likely to be comic than moving, as Andy Warhol explained with his soup can paintings. At least for a few months, the most efficient method of achieving this change of consciousness was felt by afficionados of the Underground to be the use of lysergic acid, LSD. That didn't last long; it was also possible to ruin your consciousness entirely. But the effect on music was lasting. Bands on the West Coast of the States, where the LSD fad began, started to make music to take drugs to. Also to make love to. It was called, simply, *acid rock*, and it abandoned regular rhythm and lyrical density and relied on pure sound (feedback, for example), and improvisation. One song might last half an hour, and the new popularity of LPs (most people could afford them now) meant that the work of bands like The Grateful Dead could be transcribed directly onto plastic. You didn't have to change the record over every few minutes. The new music was made for the bedroom as well as the dance floor.

So flower power dance was no mere substitute for sex. Along with the free-flowing hippy clothes, it was a way of expressing freedom from conventional restraint. You moved any way you liked, and you moved your whole body. The centre of gravity was no longer sexual. If you shook your whole body, it wasn't because you were trying to do a dance called 'The Shake', and nor was it an imitation of sexual frenzy; it was a symptom of a more general state of frenzy you were going through at that very moment. Your head was involved too, as well as your body; so you shook your head around. You didn't have to dance with a partner, and you could wander off the dance floor and re-appear ten minutes later while the band were still playing the same number. And you had to improvise, since no-one, including the band, knew what rhythm the band were going to play next. Dance was no longer an imitation, or a substitute. It was a performance in its own right. As the musicians used sound outside any rhythmic or harmonic structure, so the dancers felt that any movement was valid outside the context of an organised routine.

It didn't last long. 'Underground' dancing – free form, or idiot dancing, as it's been called – was mainly confined to student dances, 'happenings', and clubs like the Middle Earth: one big room with slide projectors playing waves of colour on the walls, down-beat disc jockeys like John Peel, and young people dressed in jeans, sneakers, scraps of gypsy cloth, transparent dresses, faces smudged with make-up and a smell of incense in the air.

The spontaneity soon became routine. Swinging London had been a commercial affair, and as its heroes went their own ways – Mary Quant, Michael Caine, Brian Epstein *et al* – they often found a safe base in the media and industries they'd transformed. Not so the flower power culture. The Movement (as it came to be called) split up into hesitant factions that could no longer sustain the euphoric gaiety and confidence of the Middle Earth days.

As hundreds of thousands of young people around the world began to see themselves as part of an international youth movement, open air festivals became the main centres of the Movement instead of small clubs like the Middle Earth or the Paradiso in Amsterdam. The whole point was to be together, to show solidarity. At the Woodstock Festival in New York State ('69), the new Eden seemed to have arrived at last. It hadn't. Later in the same year a black youth was knifed by a Hells Angels gangster who was supposed to be keeping order at the Altamont Festival in California. The Stones were on stage a few feet away, playing *Sympathy for the Devil*. The Manson murders were an even more grotesque parody of the rock culture dream.

But Altamont and Manson were only symptoms. The real problem was the inability of the Movement to agree on an answer to the challenge presented by the election of Richard Nixon in '68 and the growing US involvement in Vietnam. The Movement split between people who thought society should be changed by violent confrontation, and those who felt it should be left to destroy itself while its opponents tried to create a new society out in the fields or the desert.

The backwash of this conflict is still being felt in Britain. People are still moving out to country communes, and now you can read about them in the Sunday press. And the spirit of confrontation continues in the violence of urban terrorism. Even the music remains, in the 'heavy metal' sound of latter-day 'progressive' bands like Black Sabbath. They make your feet twitch all right, but there's no real dance, except, as Roy Carr explains, a kind of bleak parody of the Middle Earth days:

'Black Sabbath are perhaps the only band in existence who have got the non-art of their music down to a fine art. . . . With glazed eyes fixed on the stage, the seatholders rise up as one, then with arms well over their head rock backwards and forwards in slow motion like seaweed.'

That's all. There's nothing else left of the Sixties rock culture. Its radical concerns have now become a matter for everyday debate: ecology, paranoia about the CIA, the Third World. If there's a new subculture where new styles of dance may suddenly flower, it's not yet visible to the naked eye.

There's no doubt the most likely candidates are the West Indian clubs. 'Ska' had been followed by 'rock steady', softer and slower. After 'rock steady' came 'reggae', music definitely made for dancing – again born in Jamaica, a continuous nagging riff with a distinct missed beat that teases any dancer who can't really move with the music. It's not easy music for straight-hipped whites to dance well to; Desmond Dekker was its earliest exponent on TV, and his neat, tight, jerky movements are easier to parody than imitate exactly. Flick Colby suggests West Indian reggae dancing is nervous, under-stated, stylish but somehow lacking in aggressive confidence – in tune with the edgy manner of many reggae singers on *Top of the Pops*.

Many West Indians abandoned the term *reggae* years ago. Nowadays 'reggae music' – popularized by white singers like Paul Simon and Paul McCartney – has been commercialized, although a few original West Indian bands are popular with blacks and white rock fans: Toots and the Maytals, Bob Marley and the Wailers.

Reggae and the music that flows from it (simply 'the blues') is still mainly a

Top: Soul dancing in a North London Youth Club.

An outdoor pop festival illustrating the joint emotions expressed in modern dance; individual 'display', combined with a strong group identity. The latter, as demonstrated by the 'chain', echoes the Mediaeval Carole – the root of all Western dance.

West Indian domain. Some West Indian dances like 'The Rub' are so overtly sexual (actual sex rather than a substitute) that most white kids can't cope with them. But black and white kids all enjoy soul. There's no distinctive soul rhythm, and no one soul dance; although the Philadelphia stable of producers Thom Bell, Kenny Gamble and Leon Huff (the Philly Groove) has replaced Detroit's Tamla Motown as the most fashionable source of hits, many new soul records are so distinctive (Van McCoy's 'The Hustle') that they dictate new steps, new kinds of dance. The companies sell more records that way. In the North, in dance halls in towns like Wigan, many young people, black and white, take all this so seriously they've developed a soul culture of their own: *northern soul*. The really keen dancers will lock the dance hall doors late at night and practise on their own, probably without partners, working out steps of amazing intricacy and variety, all kinds of baroque movements, like carefully controlled dervishes, in quiet desperation.

Teenagers nowadays also dance to white music: T. Rex, Slade, Gary Glitter. T. Rex, who once played at the Middle Earth in the person of their main star Marc Bolan, extended the bi-sexual make-up appeal of Jagger, but their music's based on straight twelve-bar blues. Slade and Gary Glitter are the heroes of what might be called 'Glam Rock', or 'Stomp Rock': a fast, heavy rhythm reminiscent of football crowds stamping their feet and sometimes of playground chants. Slade in particular are ostentatiously working-class: (with titles like Coz I Luv You). Both dress in glittering larger-than-life costumes, as impossible to imitate in everyday dress as Gary Glitter's melodramatic stage manner. They're all stars, who're there to be idolized, rather than subculture heroes who express new trends and styles. And that's reflected in the most common way of greeting the new bands on stage: fists raised in the air, or scarves and hands waved in a football stadium ritual.

None of the other new stars have started new kinds of dance. The Osmonds are for the 'weenyboppers' – kids who're younger than teenagers and maybe even too old to go dancing anywhere except each other's homes. Groups like Mud and The Rubettes imitate old rock 'n' roll songs: Rock Nouveau. But they rarely imitate the old jive dance style. Perhaps most hostile to any new kind of dance is the 'nostalgia' boom – once seen as merely a longing for more safe and confident times. It's now becoming clear, though, that record companies have discovered that old hits still sell even if they don't have any nostalgia value: hit records can be re-released *ad infinitum*. At the time of writing there are songs from four decades in the Hit Parade. It's hard to see how any one new dance can assert itself in that context.

Popular dance since the Forties has gone through a series of radical changes. Rock 'n' roll involved almost the whole body, an unusual idea in recent Anglo-Saxon popular dance, and did away with the idea of formal steps, a dance routine. After the Twist, you could dance alone. The free form dance of the Flower Power days summed it all up. Maybe there was nowhere else to go. We're back in a more nervous, hesitant world that hardly encourages the confident expression of new dance styles. A long way still from dancing in the street.

The People's Dances

Most of this book has been concerned with the dances of the noble, the leisured, and the moneyed classes. Until very recently they dominated dance fashion. Only in the 19th century did they begin to lose their control; and not until the Fifties did the leadership return to the leisured and the moneyed. But by now they were called teenagers with a nobility of their own – the male singer, who has coloured their new fashion in dance since Elvis.

Why have we ignored the great mass of the people for so long, from the Basse Danse to the Modern Ballroom Dance? Miss Quirey explains on p.48: 'it was not where the action was'. Probably the people's dances changed far less than those of the nobility's. Some of the reels danced in Scotland and in Ireland, and until *very* recently in England, are as old as the oldest dances in the book. Yet they are still to be found today in their places of ancient origin. Probably also the labouring class needed less dances; the opportunities for a man, who worked so long in the day, to enjoy a dance were far fewer – perhaps just a few days in a year, on a celebration, or on a feast day. Dr Tom Flett speaks of a Scottish island, remote from the mainland, where only one dance was ever danced – the 4-handed reel – until a Mr Smith took a boat out in the 1890's to teach them a somewhat larger repertoire.

Probably the dances of the working people of England, Wales, Ireland and lowland Scotland have always been not unlike what are called Country Dances today; dances in circles, lines and squares, the dancing decorated by footing or step-dancing, dancing certainly of a restrained nature to the best of our belief. There is an odd feeling the the British peasant, the ancestor of today's working man, was some great hairy thing, whooping and walloping when he danced, and falling over dead drunk at regular intervals. This was in contrast to the decorous gentility of Court. It's doubtful. The jar probably passed around just as often in both environments. And any way in which we can judge the country people's dances of the recent centuries, there seems no reason to believe that they did not possess the restraint and the dignity of the British countryman. That isn't to say that there weren't wild times. . . .

As this book has already described, in the sixteenth century the people's country dances were taken into the Court of Queen Elizabeth. Very soon the dancing masters began composing further dances in the country style – figures to a lively tune, or sometimes a stately one. Very slowly, some of the livelier of the composed country dances were taken back into country places, and they became once more the country people's dances, remaining so even when the leisured classes had forgotten them. They had spread to England, Scotland, Ireland,

Wales and to New England in the United States. They became the people's dances once more. But Cecil Sharp, the great collector of folk music, song and dance, came across the dances of the Appalachian Mountains in 1917. There the dancers moved fast around a circle, sometimes altogether, sometimes grouping into fours, dancing figures and moving on, couple to couple, *around* the set. All this was to a fiddle, and to the rhythmic, chanted instructions of the leader or 'caller', usually dancing as he called. What the dancers never did was to go across the set from one side to another. They always went round it, *as if there were something in the centre*. Sharp thought that this was the oldest form of peasant dance, of English origin, that he had ever seen. (Also the speech and song of these poor, farming people, the genuine hillbillies, contained indications of English origin. The songs are often of forgotten English aristocrats, or of people on their way from 'Nottamun town'.)

What might have once been in the centre of a dancer's circle? A sacred thing? A holy bush or a tree? A church? A maypole? No one knows. But it does give us some idea of the possible origin of the country dance – in a ritual.

One sentence about that maypole. There is an English maypole, tall like a telegraph pole, and decorated at its top with a bower of flowers and short ribbons. It was set up in spring time, or remained permanently on the village green, and it was danced around. The short stumpy little thing with long ribbons, set up in a draughty school playground, where children plait the ribbons to a thumping piano or to a pre-war 78 record, and where Freddy never gets it right, but we don't like to leave him out – is a phony. It was adapted by John Ruskin, when he was a lecturer at Whitelands Training College, from some of the dances of southern Europe, and suitably modified for his young, Victorian lady students to learn and to teach. I wonder if those young ladies really knew what they were dancing round? Or Ruskin himself, for that matter, in those pre-Freudian days.

But there is one more dance form still found today that we have not mentioned in this book. In a sense it has no place in a book about popular dance, because it is for a selected few – only for men – and only for display. But it is 'popular', as village cricket, or darts in a pub, are popular, even though it is for the select of the community. For the community associates itself with the village cricket team, or the pub darts' team, and it is proud of them. We are talking of the men's ritual dances found, oddly enough, in the most advanced industrialized part of the United Kingdom, England. (There are two major exceptions to that, the Sword Dance of Papa Stour, a remote Scottish island, and the Wexford Mummers of Eire.) The best known name for these dances is the Morris. The word 'Morris' is probably a mediaeval corruption of the word Moorish; belonging to the Moors, or, that is to say, not Christian, or older than Christianity. Also, once, the Morris dancers blackened up to disguise themselves by putting their fingers up the chimney and covering their faces. Thus they looked like black men, or Moors as they were then called. The best known Morris dances come from the centre of England, in an area stretching from Oxford across to the Forest of Dean, and from the Thames up to Staffordshire (though the area was once much larger). In this part of England there is a record of about a hundred or so villages and small towns since 1800 who supported their own Morris team.

Bampton, Oxfordshire. The classic springtime Morris, the type referred to by Shakespeare. Bampton has an unbroken record of Whitsuntide dancing for over three hundred years. The village has three teams, one of teenage boys. Note the formal decorated hats, the handkerchiefs (once perhaps bunches of flowers) and the bell pads around the lower leg. The men dance in the streets in the morning and then in the gardens of the big houses in the afternoon.

The figure they are doing is called 'foot up'. It begins each dance as the team dance towards the audience.

Left: *Bacup, Lancashire.* The Royal Britannia Coconut Dancers, North Western Morris Dancing in the Rochdale Road on Easter Monday to the town band. Note the 'blooded' badge on the cap, the red and white barrelled skirts and above all the cotton bobbins on the waist and above the knees. The nearest dancer still has the hand bobbins on the back of his left hand.

The team is dancing their second dance, the garland dance, rather like a Quadrille; it may be no more than a century old. Their main dance is of a series of leaps and kicks accompanied by a tattoo on the cotton bobbins and a procession from place to place.

They are the last team to blacken their faces in the mediaeval style. The team was once composed entirely of workers of the Royal Britannia Mill.

The Morris is a seasonal dance; that is to say, it only appears historically at one particular time of the year, Whitsun. (Surviving teams now dance whenever they feel like it, but Whitsun is still the special time.) Up to the last century the men wore their own clothes (it was all they had), bedecked with as many ribbons or bright things as they could afford. If the team could wear bright, white clothes, so much the better. A beribboned and a flower bedecked hat was almost an essential. Around the lower leg were bell pads that made a ringing sound during the dancing. Bells around the legs can be found in almost every ancient dance in the world, of a ritual nature – they make a noise and clear the area of anything evil that may be around. For this is what the Morris Men are doing, purifying and defining the area in which the community lives. They also leap high in a virile way, usually, it is said, to make the crops grow. This is a form of Sympathetic Magic. But the Morris is a dance for young men, and young men are the most virile things around in the community, or they should be. The Morris is far more likely to have been a dance that was meant to encourage the *general* health, fertility and well-being of the whole of the community. One has often felt suspicious about those crops! It sounds about as sensible as going 'whirr, whirr' when your car won't start. Of course, the ritual purpose of the dance has been forgotten for centuries. Only a vague feeling associated with good luck survives. The Morris now has the same reason for its existence as any other male activity – to make an excuse for a trip out, for a few pints and, for the married man, an escape from the wife and kids – and, in the case of the Morris, for the pleasure of dancing.

The dance itself varies in style according to the village who dance it, or from where it was collected. To the casual observer, though, it's hard to detect the difference between one style of dancing and the other. To the crowd there are only two Morris dances – one where the dancers carry handkerchiefs, and one where they strike sticks. The 'mystery' of the different village styles (about thirty have been thoroughly researched) is fascinating, and a study for the enthusiast that can last all his dancing life. The general form, however, from village to village is fundamentally the same. To a strong 2/4, 4/4 or 6/8 rhythm, played at a tempo halfway between a slow and a quick màrch, the dancers perform a series of figures, interspersed with a chorus. Usually the figures in a particular village are always the same, but the chorus changes from dance to dance and gives it its character. The dances are usually to the tunes of old popular songs, the words long forgotten. For centuries the music was to a pipe and drum, called a tabor, but now it is to a fiddle or an accordion. At times the music slows down to half tempo and strong movements, known as 'full capers', different in each village, are performed. This is the nearest we come to the 'heavy', jumping peasant of mythology (though in fact he mustn't be *heavy*, however strong the movement is).

The height of popularity of the Morris, as far as we can guess, was, as with so much else, in Elizabethan times. As the railways, and education spread, and the remote country life of Hardy's novels began to break up, the Morris began to die. Many teams failed to survive the 1860's and 70's. The First World War killed off many teams in too tragically literal a fashion. Now, of the hundreds, only four survive: Abingdon in Berkshire (top hats), Chipping Campden in Gloucestershire (*no* hats), Bampton in the Bush, Oxfordshire (bowler hats) and Headington, Oxfordshire (caps). The history of Bampton is unbroken for centuries, the others have all suffered short breaks in this century.

They no longer practise at winter's end for Whitsun week and meet, dance, and fight with other teams, swopping dances and tunes, at what were known as Ales. Nor do they wander along the dusty lanes towards London, and dance in the first part of the metropolis that they came to – usually Paddington – and then return, as they had come, on foot a week later. Now they arrive at the dancing pitch by car – but they are still countrymen, and they would not call their dancing 'folk dancing'. That's for students like you and me. To them it's just 'the Morris'.

Go further North to Lancashire and Cheshire, and the Morris becomes a townsman's dance, danced by millworkers and factory workers in much more elaborate costume and in clogs. Up North there are at least eight men in the team, in two files, accompanied by a number of musicians, not the solo player of the South. Sometimes it's even the town band that plays for them. At one time it was essential to have two young boys dance at top and bottom of the files. No one knew why, but it had to be. And when the little boys got too tired, they were carried, sleeping, from one dancing spot to another. Here the men carry 'slings' not handkerchiefs – lengths of cotton, stuffed with cotton waste, like a long sausage, that can swing and make circles when you have controlled the very difficult knack. The step is brisker, more like a march. Originally the dance of the North West was a spring-time dance, as is the dance of the Cotswolds, but now it has moved to the early autumn so as to be nearer to holidays and Wakes Weeks. Only one North Western team survives to dance regularly (some get together occasionally) – at Bacup in Lancashire, the Royal Britannia Coconut Dancers, originally all workers at the Britannia Mill. Only married men were once allowed to join the team, no bachelors and no boys. They dance with cotton bobbins in their hands and strapped to their knees and waist. This is why they are called the 'coconut dancers'. And of all the teams of Western Europe they alone, in these days of High Speed Gas, and central heating, and double glazing, still blacken their faces to dance, and they appear annually in the streets of the small town on Easter Monday.

Across England, to the North East, is another Morris, though here that name is rarely used to describe the dance. The dances between the Humber and the Tweed and East of the Pennines are Sword Dances. For the Sword Dance there is a team of between five and eight men who hold the hilt of a 'sword' (which is not a real sword) in their right hand, and the point of the next man's sword in their left. To a brisk tune, sometimes a run, a circle of men weave figures with the 'swords', rarely breaking the ring. The climax comes when the swords are brought together and 'plaited' in such a way that they can be lifted and held aloft by the leader, and, in Yorkshire, they are then carried round the circle, always in a clockwise direction, the direction of the 'track of the sun around the earth'. In Durham and Northumberland, this 'lock', as it's usually called (or 'rose', or 'glass') is just held aloft and then lowered; it is not carried around the circle.

The Sword Dance was once a mid-winter dance, danced when the days were shortest. It was part of a long ceremonial play of death and resurrection. The plays have now largely been forgotten, apart from fragments. In Yorkshire the dances are for six or eight men, and the swords are made of metal, with a fixed wooden handle (except at Flamborough, where they are made of wood). The men used to wear ordinary clothes, but over the last century they have taken to dressing in a semi-military fashion (once again our Flamborough is the exception; the fishing villagers still wear their fishermen's clothes). The surviving teams are Grenoside, and Handsworth near Sheffield, and Loftus in Cleveland. Until recently there was also a team in nearby North Skelton. They stopped dancing during the First World War, but they began again during the Depression, as a means of earning a little money. They have only recently given up the

Handsworth, near Sheffield. The local version of the Long-Sword dance, performed at a jog trot. The men are circling left preparatory to beginning a figure. The costume is a Victorian invention; ordinary clothes were originally worn. The rabbit's fur on the hats is part dyed the colour of blood; the dance was once part of a long wintertime play of death and resurrection.

dance, and may well reappear again. The Flamborough *boys* appear occasionally.

Cross the Tees, and the character of the dance changes entirely, though still originally a winter-time sword dance. Now there are only five men, the swords have two handles, one of which revolves, and the metal is thin and flexible. The 'set' (i.e. the group of men) are much tighter bunched together than in the dance of Yorkshire, and the figures move much faster. Every time a figure is finished, or sometimes within the progress of the figure, the men go into bursts of simple step dancing – step, tap, tap, step, tap, tap, fast like a machine gun, to the 6/8 rhythm. The dance came to be associated with the pit villages – the dancers dressed in breeches open at the knee, as once worn in the pits for coolness; but for the dance they are made of velvet. They also have white shirts with rosettes on them, but do not wear a collar or tie. Now only Royal Earsdon (who once danced for Edward VII at Alnwick Castle, hence the 'royal') still dance regularly. Earsdon is a former pit village on the way to Blyth. Other teams have recently made sporadic appearances, notably North Walbottle and High Spen, both villages near the Tyne. Of all the display dances this is the most theatrical, because of its speed. In fact, to be truthful, it looks more difficult than it is, unlike the 'long sword dance' as the Yorkshire dances are called, which look simpler, but, in fact, are extremely demanding. But the 'rapper', as the short

Royal Earsdon, near Blyth, Northumberland. The local version of the short sword dance. Note breeches, loose at the knee, once worn in the pits. The flexible quality of the swords can be seen, and the tight knit formation of the dances. Boards are necessary for the bursts of step dancing between figures. This photograph is of the 'old' team taken in the late forties. The team now consists of their young descendants.

This dance was also a midwinter custom and once, part of a long play. Its intricate movements are very fast.

sword dance is called, can rouse a crowd in a way that only the professional companies of Eastern Europe can do – so long as the dance is well presented. The tendency has been over the last decade or so to dance it faster and faster.

When Cecil Sharp saw the sword dances of the North East he was enthusiastic for the Yorkshire dance, but not for the Tyneside rapper dance. The latter was, in his view, decadent; it had become a music hall entertainment not a ritual.

If you place the two dance styles we have talked about on a map of England, you'll see that they fall into two main regions, and leave many blanks. So far as the men's dance is concerned, there is nothing below the Thames and Severn, nothing West of the Welsh border, and nothing below the Humber in the East. This is not strictly true – there are animal dances in the Isle of Thanet (men in imitation horses' skins) and 'horses' in Minehead (Somerset) and Padstow (Cornwall). Not a man's dance, but a ritual dance, is the most famous dance of all, the 'Furry Dance' at Helston. But, by and large, the Morris lies West of the A5, East of the Welsh border, and North of the Thames and Severn. In other words, it is in the old Saxon kingdom of Mercia. The Sword Dances are found only in Danelaw. The A5 was in fact the Treaty boundary between King Guthrum the Dane and King Alfred the Saxon – except that they didn't call it the A5.

So the Morris came with the Saxons, and the Sword with the Danes and Norsemen? Perhaps, but that doesn't mean that that's how old they are in these islands. The question, 'How old is the Morris', might bring the answer, that it is as old as the time that men became farmers and not hunters, and as long as there have been young men with energy and a glint in their eyes. All the Saxons and the Danes did was to develop or alter the character of the young men's dance, just as the French did when our soldiers were in France for so long in the Middle Ages.

All that may or may not be interesting. More interesting now is whether the dance has any validity for young men, town, suburban or country of today. It seems it has. The revival of interest in the 'People's Dances' or Folk Dances began in England with the founding of the English Folk Dance and Song Society in 1911. Other societies have followed in Scotland, in Wales, and a number of smaller bodies in Ireland. After a slow start the English society has produced literally hundreds of teams of 'revivalists', spread all over the country (regardless of Danish or Saxon origins). There are even teams of excellent quality in New York and Boston. They are not interested in the history – just in the dancing, and the good fellowship. The standard is not high. A village used to have its own style, and no more; the revivalists try to study the style of all thirty, with results that aren't always pleasing. But with all the 'People's Dances', in all parts of the United Kingdom, the love and interest for them grows – not because they're old, but because they're exciting.

Table to show the development of dance form through nine centuries

Dark Ages		*Carole:* The Root dance from which all court dances developed 1. Brawls (these give us rhythms and steps). 2. Farandole (this gives us figures).	
1100			
Early Middle Ages		Estampie.	
1400			
Late Middle Ages (France) **Early Renaissance** (Italy)		French Basse Danse. Tordion. Italian Bassa Danza. Balli.	
1530			
High Renaissance (France and Elizabethan England)		Pavane Galliard Almain Coranto Volta Measures	The old and the new country dance
1623			
17th Century (France and England)		Slow Courante	The English Country Dance
1661			
18th Century (Western Europe)		Sarabande Gigue Minuet Passepieds Chaconne Pasacaille Tambourin Musette Gavotte Rigaudon Bourrée Hornpipe	English Country Dance (Later Allemande and Cotillon)

1789			
	French Revolution and Napoleonic Wars	*Cultural Crevasse*	
1815			
	19th Century (Western Europe)	Waltz Polka Quadrille Lancers Galop	
1890		Cakewalk Two step Boston Maxixe Tango One step 'Animal Dances' including Foxtrot	Ballet is now performed only by professionals as a theatrical entertainment.
1914			
	20th Century (The Western World)	*English Ballroom Dancing:* Waltz Foxtrot Quickstep Tango Latin American *1956–62* Rock 'n' Roll *1962* Twist Solo Beat Dance	Educational Dance Societies and revival societies for folk and country dance.

France			England	France			England
Louis VI	1100	1100	Henry I			1625	Charles I
Louis VII			Stephen	Louis XIV	1643		
Philip II			Henry II			1649	Commonwealth
Louis VIII			Richard I			1660	Charles II
Philip III			John			1685	James II
Philip IV			Henry III			1688	William and Mary
Louis X			Edward I				
Philip V			Edward II			1702	Anne
Charles IV			Richard II			1714	George I
Philip VI				Louis XV	1715		
John II						1727	George II
Charles V						1760	George III
Charles VI	1380			Louis XVI	1774		
		1399	Henry IV	1st Republic	1789		
		1413	Henry V	Consulate	1795		
Charles VII	1422	1422	Henry VI	Directory	1799		
Louis XI	1461	1461	Edward IV	1st Empire	1804		
Charles VIII	1483	1483	Edward V	Louis XVIII	1815		
		1485	Richard III			1820	George IV
			Henry VII	Charles X	1824		
Louis XII	1498			Louis Phillipe	1830	1830	William IV
		1509	Henry VIII			1837	Victoria
				2nd Republic	1848		
				2nd Empire	1852		
Francis I	1515			3rd Republic	1870		
Henri II	1547	1547	Edward VI			1901	Edward VII
		1553	Jane / Mary			1910	George V
		1558	Elizabeth I			1936	Edward VIII / George VI
Francis II	1559			Fall of France	1940		
Charles IX	1560			4th Republic	1945		
Henry III	1574					1952	Elizabeth II
Henry IV	1589	1603	James I	5th Republic	1958		
Louis XIII	1610						

Glossary

Anti-masque (or ante-masque)

In the later English Court masques during the reigns of James I and Charles I the serious part of the masque was preceded by a grotesque prologue performed by professionals. The object was to throw into greater relief the beauty and harmony of the masque proper.

Binary, Ternary, and Rondeau Form

Binary form has two sections of music, A and B, related thematically, and played A B.

Ternary form has two sections of music, A and B, usually contrasted, and played A B A. The 'da capo' aria is a classic example of Ternary form. Rondeau form is a development of Ternary form, with a good many possible variations. One of the most popular has three sections of music, A, B and C, played A B A C A B A. Lully wrote a famous Gavotte in this form for Louis XIV. Another variation of Rondeau form has four sections, A, B, C and D, and is played A B A C A D A.

Empathy

Comparable with sympathy but not limited to an emotional identification with another person: not just feeling *with* but feeling *into* the thing we are perceiving. Really it is the spontaneous assumption in our own nerves and muscles of the essential stress pattern of an observed object. We all know the feeling of tension we get when we look at angular, contorted modern sculpture. Even ingenious but strained-looking modern furniture sets up a similar strain in us, in contrast to the comfort and ease we feel when beholding, for instance, a Chippendale chair or the curved front of

an 18th century sideboard. It is interesting to note, among people who can afford it, how many like their dining-rooms to have furniture by Chippendale, Sheraton, or Hepplewhite. Does it perhaps help their digestions?

Enchaînement

The term used in ballet for a sequence of steps 'linked together' harmoniously. 'Allegro' refers to steps which are lively, fairly quick, and usually sprung. The opposite 'Adage' means slow movements and held poses, requiring great control of one's balance.

Posé

A step in classical ballet where the weight is transferred from the foot of a bent leg on to the pointe or demi-pointe of a rigid one. Also called a Piqué, which gives more indication of its quality.

Prosody

The study of the metrical foundations of verse, particularly the metres of classical Greek and Latin verse. It reckons the number of 'feet' in each verse (technically a 'verse' is what colloquially we call a 'line'), and the nature of the temporo-dynamic pattern within each foot. In Greek and Latin verse this pattern is quantitative or durational, consisting of long and short syllables. The most commonly known 'feet' are the Dactyl (a finger), 'long, short, short'; the Anapaest (a reversed Dactyl), 'short, short, long'; the Spondee, 'long, long'; the Iamb, 'short, long,' and the Trochee, 'long, short' (this varies in Latin). The most common line in classical verse, the

Hexameter, has six feet; the next most common, the Pentameter, has five.

The great difference between English verse and these classical metres is that we scan our lines by accent or stress, not by quantity or duration. The English language does not have its single sounds divided into long and short syllables like Greek and Latin, but we do stress certain syllables more strongly than others. The metrical feet in English have the same names, but now a Dactyl is 'strong, weak, weak'; an Anapaest 'weak, weak, strong'; a Spondee, 'strong, strong'; an Iamb, 'weak, strong' and a Trochee, 'strong, weak'. It is important to realize that if these two systems are translated into musical notation the time signatures differ: classical Dactyls and Anapaests are in duple time, but English ones in triple; classical Iambs and Trochees in triple time while ours are in duple.

Quattrocento, Early Renaissance, High Renaissance, Mannerism, Baroque, Palladianism, Rococo, Neo-classicism, and Romanticism

Terms used by Art critics and historians to denote not just different chronological periods but the styles that go with them. They are not always at the same dates in different countries, the Renaissance occurring in Italy roughly a century earlier than in places some distance away. Quattrocento is simply the Italian for the 15th century, and co-incided there with the Early Renaissance. High Renaissance is the early 16th century in Italy, the late 16th century in England and France. Mannerism is the late 16th century in Italy, Baroque the 17th century. Pallandianism is the English 18th century and Romanticism late 18th and early 19th. All very approximate and varying from writer to writer.

Rhythm

The abstract noun 'rythm' means the flow of force in the universe around us. We can see this manifested most clearly in water: the waves in the sea, or the flow of a river. The concrete noun 'a rhythm' means, in a dance context, a little sequence of stresses, varying in duration and dynamics (in length and strength), and capable of repetition. These stresses may vary chiefly in dynamics, with the durational element almost negligible, when we get a rhythm like Waltz: 'strong, weak, weak' on the 3 beats of a 3/4 bar. They may vary chiefly in duration with only a slight dynamic difference, and we have Minuet rhythm: 'slow, quick, quick, slow'.
Or they may vary in both and we get a rhythm like Polka: ti-TUM tum, tum.

Rose Adagio

A famous dance in the first act of Petipa's ballet The Sleeping Beauty, where the ballerina is partnered by four princely suitors. They each in turn support her and then let her go while she holds (or fails to hold) an attitude standing on the pointe of one foot. The audience meanwhile holds it breath until the feat is completed. Next to the thirty-two fouettés in the third act of Swan Lake it is one of the worst circus tricks in the whole ballet repertoire, and the kind of thing that Fokine spent his life trying to banish from serious dancing.

'Vital twist'

This refers to our thread of life which is cut by Atropos, the eldest of the three Fates, having been spun by her younger sisters, Clotho and Lachesis.

Booklist

Mediaeval background

LIVINGSTONE LOWES, J. *Geoffrey Chaucer* O.U.P., 1934, n.e.1944.
LEWIS, C. S. *The discarded image* C.U.P., 1964.
LEWIS, C. S. *The allegory of love* O.U.P., 1936.
DE ROUGEMONT, D. *Love in the western world* Princeton University Press, (1940) 1983.

Renaissance

BAXANDALL, M. *Painting and experience in fifteenth century Italy: a primer in the social history of pictorial style* O.U.P., 1972.
CRONIN, V. *The Florentine Renaissance* Collins, 1967.
CRONIN, V. *The flowering of the Renaissance* Collins, 1969.
SHEARMAN, J. *Mannerism* (Style and civilization) Penguin Books, 1970.
CASTIGLIONE, B. *The book of the courtier* 1528. Dent, Everyman edition 1974.
TILLYARD, E. M. W. *The Elizabethan world picture* Chatto and Windus, 1943; Penguin Books, n.e.1972.
ARBEAU, T. *Orchesography* 1588, translated by C. W. Beaumont. New York: Dance Horizons, paperback 1965; Dover Publications, 1967.
DAVIES, Sir John *Orchestra, or A poem of dancing* 1596. Chatto and Windus, 1945; New York: Dance Horizons, paperback 1970.
LEWIS, C. S. *Spenser's Images of life* edited by A. Fowler. C.U.P., 1967.
YATES, F. A. *Astraea: the imperial theme in the sixteenth century* Routledge and Kegan Paul, 1975.

17th Century

KNIGHTS, L. C. *Explorations* Chatto and Windus, 1946.
DE LAUZE, F. *Apologie de la danse* 1623, translated by J. Wildeblood. Muller, 1952.

18th Century

FEUILLET, R. A. *Orchesography, or The art of dancing* 1706, translated by J. Weaver. New York: Dance Horizons, 1970; Gregg International, 1971.
MELLERS, W. *François Couperin and the French classical tradition* Dobson, 1950; New York: Dover Publications, paperback 1968.
KITTO, H. D. F. *Form and meaning in drama* Methuen, 1959; University paperbacks, 1968.
DE MOURGUES, O. *Racine or the triumph of relevance* C.U.P., cased and paperback 1967.
RAMEAU, P. *The dancing master* 1725, translated and published by C. W. Beaumont, 1930. New York: Dance Horizons, paperback 1970.

19th Century and after

LEWIS, C. S. *De descriptione temporum* in *They asked for a paper* Bles, 1962. (His 1954 inaugural lecture at Cambridge.)
YOUNG, G. M. *Victorian England: portrait of an age* O.U.P., 1936; 2nd edn. paperback 1960.

RICHARDSON, P. J. S. *The social dances of the 19th century in England* Herbert Jenkins, 1960.

MOORE, A. *Ballroom dancing* Pitman, 8th rev. edn. 1974.

ELTON, G. R. *The practice of history* Methuen, 1968; Fontana, 1969.

STEARNS, M. and J. *Jazz dance* New York: Macmillan, 1968.

GILLETT, C. *The sound of the city: the rise of Rock and Roll* Souvenir Press, 1971; Sphere, 1971.

MABEY, R. *The pop process* Hutchinson, 1969.

The paintings on pages 46 and 69 are reproduced by gracious permission of H.M. the Queen.

Acknowledgement is also due to the following for permission to reproduce illustrations:

GEORGE ALLEN & UNWIN page 41 (from *Copernicus, the Founder of Modern Astronomy* by A. Armitage); JUDITH CRAIG page 84 (from *The Dancing Times*); EDINBURGH UNIVERSITY LIBRARY page 51; ENGLISH FOLK DANCE AND SONG SOCIETY pages 110, 111, 114 and 115; MARY EVANS PICTURE LIBRARY page 71 top, both pictures page 72; PHOTOGRAPHIE GIRAUDON page 7 (Blois Chateau photo Lauros), page 23 (Musée Condé, Chantilly), page 53 (Bibliothèque de l'Opéra), page 57 (Chateau de Versailles photo Lauros); PHOTO HACHETTE page 46 bottom (Bibliothèque Nationale); KEYSTONE PRESS AGENCY page 95, page 106 bottom; THE RAYMOND MANDER AND JOE MITCHENSON THEATRE COLLECTION page 71 bottom, page 79; MANSELL COLLECTION page 11, page 20 top, page 58 left, page 73, page 77, page 80, page 81; MUSÉES ROYAUX DES BEAUX-ARTS, BRUXELLES page 20 bottom; NATIONAL GALLERY, LONDON page 29; NATIONAL PORTRAIT GALLERY, LONDON page 6 bottom left; NATIONALBIBLIOTHEK, VIENNA page 12; POPPERFOTO page 58 right (from *The Dancing Times*), page 88; ELVIS PRESLEY APPRECIATION SOCIETY page 92 (from *Elvis Presley* by W. A. Harbinson pub. Michael Joseph); RADIO TIMES HULTON PICTURE LIBRARY page 61, page 67 top, page 82, page 85, page 94; REX FEATURES page 97; SKR PHOTOS INTERNATIONAL LTD page 102.

The top photograph on page 106 was taken by Nick Hedges and that on page 117 by Peter Pugh-Cook.

Front Cover: Detail from *Bal du duc de Joyeuse* from the Musee du Louvre Paris; dancers from Arlene Phillips at the Dance Centre, Floral Street, London photographed by Peter Pugh-Cook.

Acknowledgement is also due to the following:

FABER & FABER LTD for extract from 'New Year Letter' by *W. H. Auden*; HUTCHINSON EDUCATIONAL LTD for extracts from 'The Pop Process' by *Richard Mabey*.

Short extracts are included from:

NEW SOCIETY 20 February 1964 (Beat Gangs on Merseyside – *Colin Fletcher*); DANCE IN SOCIETY by *Frances Rust* – ROUTLEDGE & KEGAN PAUL 1969; NEW SOCIETY 15 September 1966 (The Dance Invasion – *Orlando Patterson*); 'Awopbopaloobop Alophamboom' by *Nik Cohn* – WEIDENFELD AND NICOLSON LTD 1969.

Illustration on page 8 reproduced from *Manual of Classical Theatrical Dancing (Cecchetti Method)* by Beaumont and Idzikowski, first published 1922; illustration on page 50 from WEAVER, John: *Orchesography*, translated from the French of Raoul Auger Feuillet, London 1706. Reprinted 1971 by Gregg International Publishers Limited, Farnborough, Hants, England. By courtesy of the publishers.